DIGITAL GODDESS

The Unfiltered Lessons of a
Female Entrepreneur

DIGITAL GODDESS

THE UNFILTERED LESSONS OF A FEMALE ENTREPRENEUR

VICTORIA MONTGOMERY BROWN

HarperCollins
LEADERSHIP

An Imprint of HarperCollins

Published by HarperCollins.

Book design by Maria Fernandez for Neuwirth & Associates

The names of some individuals mentioned in the book have been changed to protect their privacy.

Any internet addresses, phone numbers, or company or product information printed in this book are offered as a resource and are not intended in any way to be or to imply an endorsement by HarperCollins, nor does HarperCollins vouch for the existence, content, or services of these sites, phone numbers, companies, or products beyond the life of this book.

ISBN 978-1-4002-2062-5 (eBook)
ISBN 978-1-4002-2061-8 (HC)

Library of Congress Control Number: 2020940456

Printed in the United States of America
20 21 22 23 SKY 10 9 8 7 6 5 4 3 2 1

For Dad

CONTENTS

DIGITAL GODDESS

The Unfiltered Lessons of a
Female Entrepreneur

INTRODUCTION

Getting an EKG, an MRI, and two CAT scans of the brain was not my plan for a Tuesday in June. My calendar had contained the kind of appointments any CEO might expect—meetings with staff, a sponsor lunch, a call with one of our investors, a strategy session with my cofounder. Instead, I'd rushed to the ER, convinced I was having a stroke. Turned out it was a panic attack.

In my twelve years as a founder and CEO, time after time there have been setbacks, challenges, and real personal issues that could have quashed me, let alone the business. But I keep getting back up! Being an entrepreneur is not for the faint of heart, but it's satisfying as hell.

I've worked at many different organizations in the course of my career. None has been so challenging and yet rewarding as building and working at my own company. Time and again, I think I'm "done" with the stress and anxiety, but every time, I rally and find new motivation to continue. Fact is, as writer

Jesse Itzler points out, when you think you are done, tapped out, you are generally only 40 percent done.[1] That's the attitude it takes to be an entrepreneur—whether the business thrives, survives, or dies—it's about staying in the game. And it's worth it, no matter the outcome.

How about you? Do you like what you do, or do you hate your job? Do you wish you were building something that had more meaning to you and to others? Are you okay with the status quo of your professional life? Maybe you're content but not exactly excited about the day-to-day? If business-as-usual has become business-as-boring for you, you may want to consider being an entrepreneur and starting your own company. There will never—I guarantee, *never*—be a dull day, and each and every day will matter. Especially in the early stages.

Digital Goddess is a book for entrepreneurial women at any stage of life who want to know what it actually takes to build a business, in a world that's not always fair, predictable, or politically correct. It is one woman's story—by no means universal, but common enough to be instructive. It's about how I've dealt with the way things are, not the way I hoped things would be or the way I think they should be. It's about sucking it up, making the hard choices, and dealing with the consequences.

Today, women are starting businesses at an unprecedented rate. In 2017, 40 percent of entrepreneurs were female, and in the decade prior, the number of women-owned businesses increased by 58 percent (compared to businesses overall, which increased by 12 percent).[2] Today, women are slightly more likely to start a business than men. So, now more than ever, we need to have real conversations about issues that matter to us, both at work and at home.

I want to help catalyze those conversations and inspire more women to take the leap. In the pages ahead, you'll find a real-life account of my journey—someone who's started and run her own business and set her own culture. There's the good stuff about being a woman in business and the not-so-pretty. This is not an idealistic vision of how business "should" be; it's an honest reflection on how it is, and how it was in the not-so-distant past. I'm going to take you on a tour of the start-up world before anyone knew what "woke" was. Buckle up! I've built and run a business for more than a decade, dealt with every facet of it including investors, employees, and hell, even making payroll. That last thing? Turns out, that's actually the most daunting.

Our company, Big Think, isn't a venture-funded tech darling, born and raised in a Silicon Valley incubator. It's a scrappy, creative, labor of love that was born in a New York City bar and raised in a rented closet in someone else's office. It has had to fight for its existence most of the time. This book is not a story of eventual, massive, financial success and the building of a unicorn. It's also not one of the oft-heard stories of a company's near-demise and phoenix-like rise. (What is it with the mythical beasts in these metaphors? Or maybe that's the point—they're myths.) Anyway, that's not this story either. And yet, it's been worth it.

What Big Think has done, to my great pride, is make a real impact on people's lives and in particular on the way people think. And I'm not just talking a handful of people—we recently passed one billion views. We've featured thousands of the brightest minds in the world; partnered with elite institutions and leading-edge companies; and reached viewers and readers all over the world. Along the way, the company has dealt with all the things an average entrepreneurial venture deals with. As such, I hope its story is relatable to entrepreneurs in many different fields.

In the pages ahead, I'll talk frankly about things like getting investors, keeping them happy, hiring and firing, creating a healthy workplace culture, dealing with crises, working with a business partner, and more. I'll get personal and share the ups and downs of my romantic life while running a business; my strategies for dealing with powerful and sometimes predatory men; and the steps I've taken to better understand and manage my own mental health and well-being. And for what they're worth, I'll share some conclusions I've come to and lessons I've learned. For example, it's a mistake to think we can—or should—entirely banish sexual dynamics from the workplace. And that, since the power and the money still lie largely with men, pretending it's not that way, or being angry that it is, won't lead to success. Also, best not to wear a minidress and high heels to meet your arresting officer. Above all, that transparency is always necessary, even when it may cost you everything you've built.

The best stories are honest stories, and that is what this book offers—even when it's uncomfortable or unflattering. If there's one thing I can say about my time in business, it's that I've always been myself, even when it seemed like a total drawback. This is my raw, unfiltered story (which is pretty hilarious at times, if I do say so myself), and I hope it will challenge everything you thought you knew about being a digital goddess.

CHAPTER 1
NEVER LIE TO YOUR INVESTORS

(Even When You Just Got Arrested)

Imagine that you're a first-time entrepreneur about to launch a new business. You've got notable investors backing you; and in the coming weeks, there's going to be a major article in the *New York Times* business section featuring the company, you, your business partner, and one of your high-profile investors. And then, out of the blue, you get arrested. What do you do? Panic? Hope it goes away? Or be as transparent as possible and let your team and every investor know immediately?

That's the completely unexpected dilemma I faced in November 2007. I was walking out of New York's Union Square subway station at 8:00 a.m. when my cell phone rang. I didn't recognize the number. Typically, I only answer calls from people I know, but something told me to pick this one up. I flipped the phone open (yes, this was the era of flip phones).

"Hello?"

"Victoria, I'm a detective with the New York City Police Department. I need you to get in a cab and come to my midtown precinct immediately."

Strangely, the voice on the other end of the line sounded as if it was almost laughing. Was this some kind of joke? Had something bad happened to my sister, who also lives in New York? I asked the detective why he needed to see me. I can't recall exactly what he said, but the gist of it was that I'd wronged some powerful people and needed to come in and talk with him. Being a responsible person who'd never been in real trouble before, I hailed a taxi and did exactly as he instructed.

As we sped uptown, it occurred to me to call my dad. He asked why they wanted me to go. When I replied that I didn't know, he told me, "Get out of the car immediately. Don't even think about going until you know what it's about."

I hung up the phone but kept going. I think I was in shock. Plus, my "good girl" instinct had kicked in. I'm always someone who wants to do the right thing and please people, sometimes to my detriment. My next call was to my then boyfriend, Michael, a banker who had also trained as a lawyer. He told me to get out of the car. Nope. I kept going. I then called my cofounder, Peter Hopkins, who also told me not to go. A theme here? You bet. All reason escaped me—I was compelled to go out of fear and a total lapse of judgment. I was sure there must be some big mistake.

The taxi ride was hell, but I was strangely calm. Apparently, I have a capacity to compartmentalize in times of crisis (or maybe *disassociate* is a better term). In any case, my mind did what it had to do to get me through. I knew that I had to deal with the situation immediately in front of me and not let my feelings about it get the better of me.

Arriving at the precinct, I quickly took in the scene—several uniformed police officers milled around; a couple men in handcuffs; a number of people waiting, looking bored.

"Victoria?"

I turned at the sound of my name and saw a tall man in civilian clothes with a look of barely concealed amusement on his face. I should note that I was dressed in a gray mini-dress, pink tights, and pink high-heeled shoes. Not exactly the outfit one would choose to wear to one's (unknowing) arrest and definitely not typical attire for a police station. I acknowledged it was me, and he gestured for me to come through a side door. Looking back now, it seems so naïve, but I just followed him up some stairs to a room with, yes, a two-way mirror.

"Do you know why you're here?" he asked. I honestly told him I did not. "You upset a powerful man," he said, which left me none the wiser. "I was contacted by someone senior in the NYPD and instructed to call you in."

When he stepped out of the room for a moment, I pulled out my phone. There was next to no battery left, but I might manage one call. I called Peter and told him the updated situation.

3

"Hang tight," he said. He would call his father, a criminal defense attorney. *Hang tight?* There was nowhere I could go! Moments later, my battery down to its last few percent, Peter's father called, and I hurriedly explained the position I was in.

"Have you been arrested?" he asked.

I said no.

"Get up and walk out." My phone died before I could ask him anything further, so I gingerly stood up. The detective had left the door open (clearly, I was not a threat) and was standing outside.

"Excuse me, I think I'm going to go now." He turned abruptly and came back into the room, this time closing the door firmly behind him.

"Now you're under arrest. I won't cuff you if you remain calm." And then he sat down and mentioned a name, and this bizarre sequence of events began to make sense.

The name, which I won't repeat here, was that of my former boss, a major television journalist with his own prime-time interview show. For the sake of our story, let's call him Mr. Snider, and let's take a brief detour back to 2003, when I was a freshly minted MBA from Harvard Business School with a six-figure student loan debt and no clear sense of what the hell I wanted to do. I'd been an artsy admit to HBS, having come from the film industry in Los Angeles. Disillusioned with Hollywood, I had hoped that getting my MBA would help me change direction, but in those tough economic times, most of my classmates were lucky to be going back to the field or even to the job that they'd previously had, much less to be changing industries.

I flirted with the idea of going into consulting, but that proved not to be a good match. My friend Yael, who at the time was an engagement manager at McKinsey & Company, gave me a mock case study to tackle, but midway through she stopped me, declaring, "Victoria, the job of a consultant is to make smaller and smaller boxes around a business problem and hone in on what to do. You keep building new boxes." No fit there.

By the time graduation rolled round, I was kind of desperate. Not only did I not have a job, I wasn't even getting interviews. I had even started applying for positions that I could have gotten without my MBA—media jobs that did not touch at all on the business end of things. Inwardly, I was panicking. *I went to the best business school on the planet, and I'm going to have go back to being a Starbucks barista!* (Yes, I was a Starbucks barista post college for a short while. I make a mean cappuccino.) I didn't regret going to HBS at all, but after all the time and financial investment, somehow I'd ended up without any real job prospects and saddled with serious debt.

Stressed, depressed, and consumed with self-doubt, I moved in with my sister Winsome. I contemplated returning to Toronto with my proverbial tail between my legs and moving back in with my parents. Luckily, fate intervened when my generous sister decided to move to Italy to be with her boyfriend and allowed me to stay in their newly renovated Tribeca apartment rent free.

Time marched on, and no new opportunities presented themselves. One night I went out for drinks with a classmate from HBS who was by then working in business development for the aforementioned Mr. Snider. She hated the job. I hated being unemployed. A few weeks later, she quit and introduced me to her ex-boss. He agreed to hire me for some freelance work, which often involved meeting him at odd times for meals to discuss what I was to be working on. I was hoping to be offered a full-time job, so I kept showing up and agreeing to new projects.

Not having grown up in New York and, at that time, not being much of an intellectual, I wasn't particularly familiar with Snider, but I quickly learned that his show was synonymous with the high-powered intelligentsia in the city. He was an excellent interviewer and esteemed by his guests and audiences alike. Even people who didn't watch him said they did. The first time we met in person, following an email introduction and a series of follow-ups, was a weekend morning. He asked me to pick a place for breakfast, so I chose Bubby's in Tribeca. It was near my sister's apartment, and my twin brother had been a waiter there a couple years earlier.

Snider showed up late. Of course, I knew what he looked like, but he didn't know anything about me, except that I'd gone to HBS, a fact that seemed to mean a lot to him.

When he strode into the restaurant, there was no doubt who had arrived—at six feet, six inches, he was hard to miss, but more importantly, he didn't want to be missed. In fact, he took his time entering, giving the other patrons ample chance to recognize him and whisper to their companions. He looked around—at first I thought he was looking for me, but I soon realized he was looking to see who was looking at him. Snider, I would soon learn, lived for attention. He craved it. If people didn't notice or recognize him, he'd be in a bad mood.

That particular morning, it being a yuppie sort of crowd, there were plenty of people who knew who he was. He turned on the false modesty, along with the charm. Eventually, as he glad-handed around, I walked over to introduce myself and bring him to the table.

When he saw me, he looked pleasantly surprised. I could almost see him thinking, "Harvard *and* tall *and* attractive." Moments later, he would find out I could be charming too. Who knew that this meeting would be the start of something that would be important in the trajectory of my career, and also to the development of my professional and personal ethics?

Snider sat across from me. He's a handsome man, but what I noticed first were his eyes, which seemed dead—almost corpse-like. It was vaguely creepy to be talking to him. There was intonation in his voice, but his eyes registered nothing. The waitress came and we ordered coffee. He was flirty with her, wanting more attention. I don't remember what I chose, but he ordered pancakes. As we waited for the food, he started describing the job he was hiring for: someone to help him understand what was going on in the world each day, someone he could depend on to be an intellectual partner. He felt his current team was missing that person. I listened intently. I nodded, making solid eye contact.

There was no room to participate in the conversation—that is not the type of conversationalist Snider is. Yes, he may be renowned as an interviewer, but when it's about him, it's all about him. The food came. Pancakes were set in front of him. Snider picked up his coffee cup and poured his coffee over the pancakes. Did he think he was reaching for the syrup? Or was that how he liked his pancakes? Whatever the reason, it was bizarre. He ate the sopping wet, soggy, black coffee–flavored pancakes while continuing to talk about himself. Ceaselessly. The plate was literally overflowing with coffee, and he appeared to not even notice.

Strange eating habits aside, the meeting went well (a good meeting with Snider is one where he talks about himself and gets you to flatter him). But it takes more than one flattery session to get the job, as I later learned, and many tirades about new ways of doing things and how inept and ineffective his current team is. Every single person I know who interviewed with him over the years was told that his executive producer was lazy and was soon to be fired. Did it ever happen? Nope. She'd been with him ever since his show launched, and he kept her around, even she would say, because she knew where the bodies were buried.

Come November, I was still not officially part of his team, although he kept asking me to do this and that. I finally gave him an ultimatum of sorts and said I needed to know if I was going to be hired full-time. It was the night before Thanksgiving, and he asked me to meet him after he finished taping that evening to discuss my future. "Where should we meet?" he asked. My family was in town, and we had dinner plans, but I'd come too far to jeopardize my job prospects now. Knowing that Snider would be recognized most places in the city, I chose a dive bar in Tribeca called Puffy's Tavern. I didn't want him distracted by fans

We were supposed to meet around six, but it was well past seven when he rolled up in a Mercedes and parked *Dukes of Hazzard*–style outside the bar. He strode in, clearly expecting people to recognize him. Not in this place! I had saved us seats in a "quiet" part of the bar. After greeting me, he went to the bar and ordered two glasses of red wine. He chugged his, reached over and chugged mine, and then ordered two more. Now he was ready to talk. On Thanksgiving Eve, after many months of job seeking, I finally had an offer.

I started the following Monday, and my first assignment was to show up at his apartment in the early morning and review the news with him. That didn't last long, as he had a tendency to lose interest in things quickly. I was grateful to have a job, but this was not where I wanted to be. I'd intended to get some real "business" experience before striking out as an entrepreneur, not to end up as a glorified production assistant for a media celebrity. (Later, I'd come to see it as a blessing that I didn't get hired by McKinsey, Goldman Sachs, or some other notable organization. Had I gotten the kind of job HBS grads dream of, I might still be there, golden handcuffs and all.)

My new role was ostensibly in business development but I ended up also being a producer. I was very good at identifying and booking guests for my boss's show, and I had a knack for identifying topics that would resonate with people. I was also good at getting the shows sponsored.

All these talents would be absolutely critical to my future, although I didn't know it at the time. Over the next two years, I produced segments featuring household names in entertainment, fashion, politics, and business, and was even nominated for an Emmy.

My relationship with Snider was a strange one. I think early on he'd developed some sort of fascination with me. I was attractive and yet wasn't in any way leading him on. I was not afraid of him (at least, back then) and could hold my own. I didn't kowtow, and I made him laugh. I was confident and sometimes brash, and I think he actually enjoyed being around me—evidenced by the fact that he came to both of my birthday parties while I worked for him, and he took me on pretty much all of his outside speaking engagements for more than two years, using me as his speech writer and producer for important business events. I felt he respected my intelligence. It was a strange relationship—one based on respect, but also him trying to get close to me in some way, beyond work.

His driver once told me, "Snider and I talk about you and we both agree, you are the prettiest, smartest, and nicest girl on the staff." I'm not sure I was any of those things, but I did keep him on his toes. And he liked it.

After about six months, I also became Mr. Snider's de facto recruiter, especially of Ivy League graduates. My boss was obsessed with Harvard, so I often advertised positions directly at the college. In the late spring of 2004, we were looking for a politics producer. I'd narrowed the search down to two Harvard guys, Luke and Peter Hopkins. I met with both over the phone and determined Peter to be the right candidate. I was impressed by his intelligence and his big, booming voice, and recommended to Snider that he meet Peter in person. That interview took place at Snider's home and, as usual, involved watching some of his interviews with famous people and complimenting his work nonstop when he wasn't busy complimenting himself. Peter told Snider that he'd told his father that, someday, he'd like to do what Snider did. When he said goodbye and walked down the steps, Snider opened the door again and said, "Tell your father someday, but not any time soon."

Snider met with Luke, too, and then accidentally hired him rather than Peter—he'd wanted to choose the person I recommended but got it wrong. I think he was also probably charmed by Luke's English accent. Once I pointed out his error, he hired Peter too. When he arrived on his first day at the show, I hadn't met him in person so didn't know what to expect. He was tall, good-looking, super-fit, gay, and we immediately hit it off. We are both driven, both funny (at least I like to think so) and we "get" each other. We're also both creative and love that process. Little did I know that Peter would become the most important professional relationship in my life for more than fifteen years and a personal one too.

Peter and I became fast friends and creative collaborators before becoming business partners. Our first collaboration was on a spoof website called "WASPDate," which chronicled the fictitious dating life of wealthy WASPs (yes, a spoof about white Anglo-Saxon Protestants) in New York City. It was picked up by *AM New York* (a free daily newspaper), and we were actually asked to write a book about it. We kept ourselves incognito. I tried to sell it to the owner of Jdate (a Jewish dating website), but he was not interested. From there, we wrote a TV pilot about a has-been, alcoholic journalist—a little in the flavor of *30 Rock* before *30 Rock* existed. On our first creative TV effort, we actually got pitch meetings with NBC and CBS. Not bad for serious rookies! During these projects, we learned we were good collaborators and brought out talents in the other. As time moved on, working together both at the show and in these external projects, we began to talk about opportunities we saw on the internet.

In particular, we saw a dearth of thoughtful content, especially in video form. This was the very early days of You-Tube, and to be frank, there was a lot of crap out there. You couldn't just go online and watch a TED talk back then. The television content we were producing was serious and sub-stantive, but it was usually tied to the issues of the moment. Late at night in the little studio apartment I was renting, we dreamed up possibilities. An online university (a novel idea back then)? Too complicated. But what if we could find a way to create a repository of smart, educational, evergreen video content that would have ongoing value? What if we could get exceptional people to distill their knowledge and expertise in a form that would stay relevant beyond the changing news cycle?

"It would be like Davos, but for everyone!" Peter exclaimed. I loved this concept—the kind of content usually reserved for that elite conference, the World Economic Forum, in the Swiss Alps, available to anyone with a computer Davos democratized. The world's best thinkers and doers made accessible to the rest of us. Everyone with whom we shared our idea was immediately struck by its resonance. Fast forward a few months, and we'd secured $1.4 million in funding for our fledgling company, which we were now calling Big Think (more on how we raised that money in Chapter 2). It was time to quit my day job and jump in with both feet, so I gave Mr. Snider my notice. Initially he was very supportive. Indeed, he hosted a small going-away party for me in the office on my last day. Some wine was consumed. People toasted me. Snider asked: "What are you going to miss most about working with me. The show? The job?"

"The car service!" I replied, only half joking. Little did I know that my throwaway remark would almost get me thrown in jail a year later.

"Car service." I looked at the detective blankly. He'd just informed me that I was potentially being charged with theft—grand larceny, to be precise. When I asked him what I had allegedly stolen, this was his cryptic response. Seeing my obvious confusion, he elaborated.

"You allegedly continued to use the corporate car service of your former employer after your employment was terminated."

In an instant, my parting words on the day I handed in my notice came back to me. I was starting to understand. Yes, I had occasionally used the car service, but that was because I'd continued to do small tasks for my former employer, figuring that the relationship was worth continuing even though I was no longer on his payroll. It certainly wasn't something that should have made it to criminal court. With the demands of getting the new venture off the ground, however, I'd not had time for him recently. So this wasn't really about the car service. This was payback for the withdrawal of my service. Clearly, he was not happy about losing my time and attention. I can only speculate about how he managed to get city officials to have me arrested. Now I understood why the detective had sounded like he was laughing when he called me. It was truly ridiculous. It was also truly scary to see such crony justice at work in this day and age.

Eventually, I was allowed to leave the police station, having been given a desk appearance, and was told that I'd receive a notice on how things were to proceed. As I sat on the steps waiting for my ride, looking down at my pink shoes, there was only one question on my mind: What on earth was I going to say to our investors? I thought raising the money was the hardest thing I'd ever done (more on that later). But this was worse.

The temptation was to keep quiet, tell no one, and hope I could deal with the situation behind the scenes. To compartmentalize my suddenly messy personal life away from my business. After all, this had nothing to do with our new venture.

But a voice in my head told me, *No. These people have invested in you. You must be completely truthful and lay things out exactly as they are.*

Arriving back at the "office"—in reality, a small alcove I shared with Peter outside the makeshift studio we built in what was once a storage closet—I was terrified. My entire reputation was at stake, as well as the future of the company we'd worked so hard to create. What if our investors pulled out? What if the *New York Times* got wind of my arrest and reported on it in the article? What if Big Think fell apart before it even launched? Would I ever be able to get a job again? Above all, I was overwhelmed by the fear of letting down people who had invested in *me*.

We shared the floor with another company, so the only place I could get any privacy to make my calls was the storage room. By this point, everybody in the office knew what was happening, but I didn't want an audience. Sitting on a filing box, hands shaking, I dialed our lead investor, David Frankel—a very successful entrepreneur. He and I had been to HBS together and he'd been the first person to take a chance on Big Think when it was little more than an idea. I thought it best to be as direct as possible, no window dressing.

"Hello?"

"David, it's Victoria."

"Hi, Victoria."

"David, I wanted to personally let you know that I was arrested recently by a very senior detective in New York City for theft of car service. The prosecution wants to charge me with grand larceny. David, you have my word that I will get through this and the launch of Big Think will continue."

It sounds like I was confident here. Not at all. But I put myself in his shoes and thought, *Hell, if I just invested close to $1* *million in a person and a business idea, I'd want that person to sound confident.* So I did.

My heart was beating out of my chest and my palms were sweaty. I was prepared for the worst. I was expecting anger and outrage and also a complete removal of faith in me. Not so. To my surprise, David was nothing but supportive. He listened and gave me advice. He offered his support and encouragement. He also assured me that he understood the person I was dealing with in Snider and the power he had.

In moments like these, it's easy to be myopic. It's useful to remember that every entrepreneur—hell, everyone—has had some major setback or embarrassment at some point in their life, and people tend to be sympathetic. Even something that seems like a disaster to you might not look so bad to someone else, especially a seasoned businessperson. Talking to David gave me some much-needed perspective.

After David, the next person on the list was Larry Summers, former secretary of the Treasury in the Clinton administration, president of Harvard, and world-renowned economist (he would later become chief White House economist under President Obama and so much more). This was the call I dreaded most. Larry is perhaps the smartest person I know and at that time was deeply intimidating to me. Not only had Larry entrusted us with his money; he was also the linchpin of the forthcoming *New York Times* article that was supposed to catalyze our launch. Without him, there wasn't a story.

We decided that Peter should be the one to call Larry, because he'd secured Larry's investment. I coached him on what to say and assumed things would go badly. It was almost worse to listen to him saying it than having to say it myself. I felt sure the future of the company was in real jeopardy. There was no way Larry would want to be involved once he heard what was going on before we'd even launched. To my great surprise, however, he was not fazed. He too knew something about the personality of the individual behind my arrest and expressed his surprise but no anger. He was still on board. And he was concerned about me.

This was my first real lesson of entrepreneurship. Transparency at all costs. I believe that this totally unexpected and seemingly disastrous event in fact increased our investors' trust in me—even before it was resolved. In that moment, and through all of the ups and downs that have followed, I have operated with full transparency on every issue I or the company has faced that would affect their investment. Transparency is nonnegotiable.

So often, I've seen people lose the trust of their investors because they embellished the good news and were not immediately forthcoming about the bad. Avoidance is the enemy. Deal with the situation immediately. I'd be willing to bet that Elizabeth Holmes, the infamous founder of the fraudulent and now-defunct medical tech company Theranos, would not be in the situation she is now if she had had the courage (and moral compass) to fess up to her impressive roster of investors that she didn't have a viable product or any real path to it. Instead, she feigned ignorance and doubled down on her lies, leading to the well-documented collapse of the company and her own current legal troubles.

People (mostly) want other people to win. In times of failure, being as open as possible, even with bad news, builds trust rather than erodes it. Yes, at that moment they may be upset, even deeply so, but in the long term, in business and in life, relationships are maintained and strengthened by honesty. I know many entrepreneurs who have gone out of business and lost their investors' money but were transparent the whole way and even secured investments in their next ventures from the same investors. Why? No bait and switch.

On that day in late 2007, still reeling from the arrest, I was beginning to learn this critical lesson. After David and Larry, I had other calls to make, and Peter had a few too. Every initial investor in Big Think needed to know. That meant Peter Thiel, founder of PayPal and first investor in Facebook, as well as Tom Scott, founder of Nantucket Nectars. Peter Hopkins took the call with Peter Thiel, who couldn't have cared less. Much bigger fish to fry. Tom Scott thought it was ridiculous and was scared for me. I was totally open about it all with the investors, and they had my back. Surprise. Big surprise. And relief. Our investments were safe, at least for now. But everything else in my life felt like a mess.

Peter's dad had given me an introduction to his friend, Peter Schaffer, a criminal defense attorney accustomed to representing murderers, rapists, massive drug dealers, or some combination of the above.

When I first met him at his office in the Bronx, my criminal defense attorney (what a crazy thing to even say!) thought I was joking with him. "Uh, this is not for real," he said.

I assured him it was and told him my theory of how "some powerful men" had been called into action to get the deed done. It was no joke.

There was a defined period (before Christmas that year) during which the plaintiff had time to decide whether he wanted to pursue the case. I had fond hope that the answer would be no, considering the whole thing was so petty and ridiculous. Surely my former boss had made his point. My friends were completely shocked at what was happening to me. Could this really be the way things worked in the United States in 2007? In the few weeks after the arrest, I got paranoid. I had a friend over, and we literally walked through the apartment looking for bugs. When I'd been at the police station, the detective had shown me pictures taken by the police or maybe the car service of my office and my home. Were they still watching me? For use of car service? We're not talking murder here, folks.

Sometimes I look back and think it's amazing I didn't have a nervous breakdown. The stress of my legal situation, on top of the everyday stress of launching a company and dealing with investors, felt unsustainable. I was in a new home, a new business, a new relationship, and undergoing a new introduction to New York's terrifying legal system. New all around. As Christmas approached, I could not get the case out of my mind. Yet I had so many other things to focus on, including launching our website and making sure there was content on it.

In the hopes of preventively addressing the issue of my arrest before our launch, we tried to hire a notable crisis public relations person—a real pro who'd dealt with all sorts of crazy business scandals. When she learned about who was involved, she decided not to take us. A crisis too big for the crisis PR firm. I actually thought she was joking. Isn't this, like, your specialty? So, it was on to the next.

Eventually we found a PR person who was adamant we should use the arrest as a point of interest for the launch of Big Think. Peter agreed with her. All publicity is good publicity, right? Wrong, for me anyway. I wanted Big Think's launch to be positive news for its own sake, not tabloid fodder because its Harvard Business School CEO had been arrested. It was a daily battle. The whole month after my arrest was painful, scary, and surreal. I felt alone. I felt like my world was coming apart. In some ways, it was.

I'm someone who always seems in control, but inside, I was falling to pieces. I couldn't stop obsessing over the future. What would happen to me? What would happen to the company? Would the investors hate me? Would I be ruined professionally for the rest of my life over something stupid? The power that my former boss was wielding over me was completely uncalled for and terrifying. It put a strain on every relationship I had—my friends, my family, my love. I became self-centered and no fun to be around, reliving the arrest over and over. I was positive about Big Think and encouraging to our team, but to anybody who was personally close to me, I was misery.

So, did I go to jail? Are you reading a book by a felon? No. Here's how it played out. My former boss refused to drop the case. Eventually, after many trips to court, accompanied by a criminal defense attorney who thought the whole thing was a joke, I negotiated a plea deal in which I'd serve two days of community service and have no record, even of the arrest. The district attorney was actually surprised that the case had even come that far. Heck, there were serious criminals out there and that even a little of the court's time and resources were taken up by this case seemed off. The experience helped shape my understanding of how power can work sometimes. I learned, quickly, how to deal with intense unfairness and navigate through it personally, without destroying the brand we were building and affecting our team. Compartmentalization, I discovered, is an essential leadership skill—and one that would serve me well in the years to come. I also learned that seemingly small decisions can have big consequences. Even things that seem inconsequential in the moment, like taking a car service, can come back to bite. Hard.

REFLECTIONS

- ◆ Integrity is critical. Do whatever you can to build and preserve your integrity, and surround yourself with people who require it.

- ◆ Small things matter. Don't underestimate that what you do on a day-to-day basis can come back to bite you. If it feels wrong at all, don't do it.

- ◆ Own up to your mistakes immediately. Be completely transparent with those who have invested in you and your business. You can actually turn the situation into an advantage by building trust.

CHAPTER 2

WHO GOES FIRST?

Raising Capital Before
You Have Any

In 2017, just 2.2 percent of all venture capital in the United States went to companies founded by women.[1] Ask female founders about their experience approaching potential funders (who are overwhelmingly male), and you'll hear story after story of bias, sexism, or worse.

A *Fast Company* survey in 2018 reported this actual quote from a venture capitalist to a female founder: "Oh, honey, your numbers look great. Who did them for you?"[2] Another woman was told in no uncertain terms that she was "too female, too old, even too blonde." Others told tales of how pitches turned into unwanted dates. Raising capital is a huge hurdle for any entrepreneur, but there's no doubt that it's that much bigger for women. Women even get asked different questions than men during investment pitches, one study found: women were more likely to be asked "prevention questions," which relate to issues of risk, safety, and potential losses, while men were asked "promotion questions," which relate to achievements, hopes, and ambitions.[3] The result, not surprisingly, was that the women got less funding. I guess I'm lucky I didn't know the bleak statistics when Peter and I started Big Think. I just knew we needed money, and I was going to need to ask for it.

I won't lie to you: it helped that I'd been to Harvard. Anyone who tells you it doesn't matter where you went to school or who you know is lying to you (and maybe to themselves). My Harvard MBA may have felt like nothing more than a very expensive piece of paper when I was contemplating taking that barista job, but when I set out to start a company, it sure came in handy. It came with two things that made a huge difference: credibility and connections.

In the summer of 2006, Peter and I had begun forging a plan while we were still working for Mr. Snider. One of my HBS friends, Liam (now a renowned tech tycoon), had recently sold a company in which a mutual classmate, David Frankel, had invested. I had been in a class with David in our second year at HBS and remembered him as being very smart and very tough. Before business school, he was the guy who brought internet service to South Africa, and he went on to become an extremely successful venture capitalist. Honestly, I'm not sure why he went to HBS; he was already an entrepreneur. But I'm sure glad he did! I decided David should be our first target, so I reached out to Liam in the hope that he'd make a (re)introduction.

Liam and I met at a diner on 57th Street, and he told me about his business and how he'd worked with David to get it started. I told him about our idea—at that point, we still didn't have a name for it. Liam agreed to reach out to David and suggest we meet. Since David is a professional investor, Peter and I knew we had to put together some sort of a deck—but neither of us had ever built one, so we asked friends what we needed to include. Side note: here's something major that HBS taught me. You don't need to know how to do things, you need to know how to ask people to do things for you. This is something at which I excel. No hubris. I don't hesitate to say, "I don't know how to do this, but you do—please help!" So, with more than a little help from our friends, we assembled our slides. The result was basic, to say the least, but it included the key ideas. Finally, we got a meeting with David—via phone. Our hopes were not too high, but we were able to get him to promise that he'd invest if—and this was a big *if*—others invested too.

. . . .

Here's something major that HBS taught me. You don't need to know how to do things, you need to know how to ask people to do things for you.

. . . .

We knew something about how this process worked. I'm sure you've seen those movies where someone's kid or wife gets kidnapped, and a meeting is arranged to hand over the ransom. Both parties stand in some dark, creepy parking lot or under a highway overpass and play the "Who goes first?" game. The bad guys want their hands on the cash before they'll give up their captive. The desperate father/husband wants to know they're really going to release his loved one before he hands over the suitcase containing all his worldly wealth. Because neither knows if he can trust the other, they have to find a way to make both things happen at once.

When raising money for a start-up, you also have to play the "Who goes first?" game. There are no bad guys here (hopefully) but the dynamics of trust are delicate. Investors may be interested, but no one wants to be the first to say *yes*. No one wants to end up the only investor, so no one wants to be first. They want someone else to commit, then they'll follow. But that "someone else" is also looking for someone else to write the first check. Like a hostage negotiator, you have to figure out how to get two people to commit simultaneously.

Getting the first investor feels impossible, but if you can pull it off, getting the second is sometimes surprisingly easy. If the right people are already on board, some investors won't even bother to do their due diligence at all—as demonstrated in the now-infamous Theranos story, where a who's who of reputable, influential funders (including legendary VC [venture capitalist] Tim Draper, Walmart's Walton family, and Rupert Murdoch) backed the fraudulent medical tech company without seeing any audited financials or peer-reviewed data, based largely on the fact that others were doing the same. We certainly weren't Theranos and had no interest in fooling anyone into backing us, but we also weren't naïve about how such things work. If you want to get investors to back an unproven business, your biggest challenge is to get someone to go first and give everyone else the confidence to follow.

This was the task facing Peter and me as we strategized about how to raise the funds to start Big Think. We knew David was interested, but he wasn't going to go first unless he knew we had others committed. Who else did we know? It needed to be someone who not only had the cash, but also had the credibility to give David confidence. Someone with a big name. High on our list because he checked all these boxes was Larry Summers. At Harvard, Peter had written an article in *The Crimson* about Summers, and he thought he'd made a good impression. Sure enough, Larry agreed to a meeting in Boston.

There's an old business adage that's turned out to be true for us time and time again: "Ask for money and you'll get advice; ask for advice and you'll get money." When Peter met with Larry, he just shared our idea and asked him what he thought. He really liked the idea and he told Peter he'd like to invest. This was a big win—almost. Larry didn't want to go first either. He told Peter he would only invest if others invested. Now we had Larry and David in position, but we still had to orchestrate the simultaneous commitment.

Still, we were elated. To be able to say that Larry Summers intends to invest in your as-yet-nonexistent start-up is wild. And maybe it would be enough to persuade others. I went back to David and told him that Larry was interested in investing. Thank goodness, that meant something to him. Something big. Larry is so well respected and so smart that people want to be associated with him. David, like me, appreciated the Harvard brand, and having the president of the university investing alongside him was meaningful, not just in monetary terms, but in terms of prestige.

That's another important lesson I've learned about raising capital: optics matter. Sure, people invest because they like the idea, or because they respect the founders or the team, but they also invest because of the other investors with whom they'll be associated.

We now had our anchor investor in David, which meant we had Larry too. Next, I went to Tom Scott, founder of Nantucket Nectars, the juice guys. He and Tom First created a company on Nantucket in the early nineties, going boat to boat to sell their juice. It became a big business and was eventually sold to Cadbury Schweppes. I'd written to Tom Scott over the years, because I was impressed by what he'd achieved—the bootstrappy-ness of it all. The earliest time I reached out (he doesn't even remember this) was when I was at McGill University in Montreal. I told him that I could help him penetrate the Canadian market by creating "Bay of Fundy Nectars." I didn't hear back from him, but I persisted. This was perhaps my first inkling that I would be an entrepreneur. Come up with an idea, pitch it, and keep going, whether or not it pans out.

Tom went on to run Plum TV—an enterprise that focused on holiday living in the Hamptons, Vail, Aspen, Miami, Martha's Vineyard, and Nantucket. While I was working for Mr. Snider, Peter and I collaborated on a few TV pitches (well ahead of their time, I think): "Faboo," a gay man's guide to these havens of the wealthy elite, and "Summer Help," about the nannies and other household staff who work for the wealthy families. I pitched them to Tom, who loved the ideas. By this time, I'd developed a bit of a rapport with him (today he's a close friend) and he entertained my pitches whenever I reached out. So, when the idea for Big Think came up, he was receptive. He'd been going through a bit of a rough patch at Plum and was perhaps eager for some sort of positive distraction. Like the others, Tom was interested but wouldn't take the lead. He, too, promised to invest if others did.

In tandem, we were also pursuing billionaire investor and PayPal founder Peter Thiel—another big name who might entice others if we could get him to commit. We had a small connection—Peter had met him in our television days—and were hopeful that would be enough to get him to sit down with us. It was. Getting him to actually back Big Think seemed like a crazy pipe dream. But at least we were going to pitch him!

The ability to get a meeting is absolutely critical for the would-be entrepreneur. You have to find even the most tenuous points of contact and turn them into a solid connection that distinguishes you from the dozens of other people clamoring for attention. Our Harvard background was often an important asset for us in this regard. Peter's connections in the gay community proved to be another. Mutual friends. Shared interests. Family. Use whatever will get you in the door.

Thiel's door, in this case, was the very grand entrance to the Bloomberg Tower, a new luxury building on Lexington at 59th Street that was the "it" place to live in those days—as evidenced by the fact that Beyoncé and Jay Z had an apartment there. At the appointed time, nervous and excited, we were welcomed into Thiel's enormous residence, with its sweeping views of the city. He sat on a chair opposite Peter and me, and we told him about our concept and who else was potentially involved. He liked the idea and was impressed by our list of reputable possible investors. We were convincing! He agreed to invest alongside the others.

We now had $1.4 million committed. We just had to close. Who knew that this was where even greater challenges would arise? A commitment does not necessarily mean it's a fait accompli—there's still paperwork to do. And, more important, you have to get people to actually wire the money. Again, you have to play the "Who goes first?" game. Oh, and you need a lawyer. It's a strange irony when you have $1.4 million promised, but you can't afford the attorney you need to close the deal. Peter and I knew we were simply unqualified to do the paperwork ourselves, and frankly I'm not sure that the potential investors would have worked with us if we tried. Luckily, through a friend, I was introduced to Kiril Dobrovolsky, an attorney who was working at Orrick in San Francisco. It turns out that some attorneys are allowed to take on clients who currently do not have the means to pay, but they believe have a good shot at being funded.

In the autumn of 2006, I called Kiril. The voice on the other end of the phone sounded like a radio broadcaster. Feeling decidedly less polished, I told him about our plans and potential financial commitments. He heard me out and said that, based on my contacts, HBS education, and our verbal commitments, he would work with us until we had raised money to pay him back. He was confident we could do it.

Persuading people to believe in you and giving them confidence that you're serious are absolutely critical in the early stages of a new venture. And that's no small task for a first-time founder with no track record to show. Part of it comes down to self-confidence, without question, and communication skills. But sometimes, no matter how articulate you are about your idea, words are not enough. If there's one thing you can do to demonstrate, in action, that you're serious about your start-up, it's this: quit your day job.

TAKING THE LEAP

Quitting your day job is a major leap of faith. It's tempting to leave it as late as possible—to wait until you know your start-up idea has funding and has gained some momentum. But, guess what—people don't like to fund things if the entrepreneur and CEO don't have their entire skin in the game. You better have something big to lose, or how are people going to believe you are all in? For your would-be investors and other stakeholders, knowing that you're committed full-time can be critical to sealing the deal, giving them confidence that you're serious. And I'm not going to lie, I think that it's likely even more important for women to show that they are all in. From the investors' perspective (perhaps unjustifiably so), it's a risky enough concept to invest in a female founder, so she had better show that she's totally committed and will stop at (nearly) nothing to get it done. After months of coming up with ideas and talking with people about them, it was clear to me that I needed to take that leap. The venture had to be my professional priority and my sole focus. Everything else needed to be put aside.

"We need momentum," I told Peter one day after we got off a series of calls with potential investors. Without a sense of urgency, things would dawdle along for ages. I put myself in the investors' shoes. If I were an investor, what would it take to get me to write a significant check to someone I didn't know very well, who had never started a business before? Would I invest in someone who still had a job that required working long hours and paid her enough to keep her comfortable? No. I'd want to see that she had something to lose and actually needed to make the start-up a success.

In sales, it used to be said that the best hires were men who had young kids and a wife to support. They had no option but to make the sale; otherwise they could not support their families. I thought about this when starting Big Think. Yes, our investors needed to be intrigued by the idea and see its potential to succeed and to scale, but they also needed to see that I was actually in a place of discomfort if it didn't work out. In other words, I would do whatever I could, within reason, to make the business work. And that meant I had to quit my day job.

But when? Every paycheck mattered to me, as did my health insurance. Nevertheless, I sensed that if I had things to fall back on, it would be far less likely, or maybe not even possible, that I would succeed in starting Big Think. If you have a backup, it's too easy to coast. So I gave myself a deadline. I told myself I would quit my TV production and business development job working for Snider before the end of 2006. Then I told other people too—people whose opinions mattered to me. I wrote it down and committed to it mentally.

The year rolled on. Thanksgiving came and went. Then it was Christmas. In the final few days of 2006, from an internet café near the beach in the Dominican Republic, where I was spending the Christmas break with my then boyfriend, I emailed Snider my resignation. I'd told people I would, and I did.

I had no other form of income lined up and no savings. I was all in. This start-up had better work or else. For me, this was a necessary approach. Had I not given myself a deadline, time might have slipped away, and it would have been far more comfortable to wait and quit my job when things were lined up more securely. But if you truly want to start something—whatever it may be—waiting won't help. Take the leap to commit now. This moment. The sooner you give yourself a deadline to start, the more likely it is to happen. For a start-up, or any venture, you need to be entirely committed. Speak as though you are already doing it. As you think, so shall it be. And put yourself in a position where you *must* do it.

The two steps I took—committing to yourself, then committing to others—are critical. Shame's a bitch, and none of us wants to feel it. As Brené Brown has said, "Shame is the most powerful master emotion. It's the fear that we're not good enough."[4] A feeling I've felt repeatedly. In this instance, I confronted it and used it as a tool. Not delivering on my commitment to myself and to others would leave me feeling ashamed. I understand that shame has been one of my negative drivers throughout my life personally and professionally, so in this instance, I used it to my advantage. This was a power move against myself!

The confidence game didn't stop with the investors. An idea is great, but oftentimes, before people invest, they want to see not only that others are investing, but that you can actually do, even minimally, what you say the company is going to do. We had to prove that we could actually attract experts to be featured on Big Think, before a website even existed.

It was time to play "Who goes first?" yet again. I suppose this happens any time you're trying to get multiple people to commit to something. Peter and I identified a small group of experts who we thought would be compelled by our mission—people who wanted to educate and help others. Our first few outreaches were to Richard Branson (we guessed his email address), musician Moby (a friend had his email address), Buddhist scholar (and father of Uma) Robert Thurman, and notable architect Lee Mindel, who works for the likes of Sting, George Soros, and many others.

Their questions were just what you'd expect.

"Who's done it before?"

"Uh, no one. We are reaching out to a very select, initial group of experts to kick-start it." See how I did that? Turned a seeming negative into a positive.

"Where's your website?"

"We are in the process of building it, and you will be featured heavily when we launch. We will issue a press release and, with your permission, you will be identified as key to Big Think. We'll say we couldn't have started it without your support." People love to feel needed, critical even.

And, of course: "Who else have you booked?" This is where gamesmanship comes in—it's not exactly lying, but it is a bit of poker bluffing. We had a few tentative yeses, but no guarantees. We didn't have filming dates on the books; hell, we didn't even have a studio or camera equipment or a producer or someone to shoot it. By words alone, we convinced these busy, in-demand people to participate. Positioning is everything.

A big part of starting a business is wrangling things without any resources to prove that you can get stuff done with very limited means. And it continues when you actually do get funded. It's occurred to me that we may have been fortunate to not have raised a lot of money at the start. (The figure $1.4 million may sound like a lot, but believe me, it's not much to get a business off the ground.) Why? Because so many companies with a long runway burn through cash and don't feel the pressure to get a product out the door. No such situation for us. Using our initial funding, we had to build a website, book talent, shoot and edit interviews, create written content, and keep it ongoing. We traveled on shoestring budgets and learned to get every last scrap of meat from the carcass. I have so much more respect for entrepreneurs who have done things with finite resources than I do for those who have had massive funding.

IT AIN'T OVER TILL THE CLOSING

Prior to securing funding, I spent a lot of time on the phone with our attorney, Kiril, getting everything in order in preparation for a closing. I also stayed in close contact with our prospective investors and kept them abreast of where we were in the process. Having their buy-in and excitement was critical. At any moment one of them could have walked away. And a couple did, at the last minute. That's not uncommon. So many times I've heard of deals falling through because of a last-minute bail from an individual. And that's totally their prerogative—it just sucks to be on the other side of it. You've got to be prepared for these setbacks. Always ready to pivot, pitch, and find another interested party. Even though we had a group of investors lined up. I never stopped pitching Big Think until we were actually funded. I was always working out contingencies.

Three months after I left my day job, we got our first round of funding. Getting all the documents together and everybody to sign and agree to a closing date was one of the craziest processes I've ever experienced. We had to get everyone to sign on the same day: April 7, 2007. By the evening we had all the signatures necessary except for Tom Scott's. I was literally calling him every fifteen minutes and got Peter to call him too. If it went past midnight, I'd have to send everyone the documents again with new dates, and that was the last thing I wanted to do. Finally, around 9:00 p.m., we managed to track down Tom and implore him to sign. Thank God he did. Peter and I could hardly believe it. After all these months of uncertainty, we were being given a chance to make Big Think a success. Our cherished idea now had capital behind it. We were our own bosses—and soon we'd be other people's bosses as well. As we drank a toast to our future at a bar near my apartment, I could hardly believe that, just a few months earlier, I'd still been working for somebody else.

When the money was wired to the bank, I was both elated and terrified. One mission was accomplished! Now the actual work could begin. Getting funded seems like the hardest thing to do, but once you have funds, you actually have to go out and build something. *Shit be real now*, I thought grimly. Perhaps this is a necessary trait for me as an entrepreneur—as soon as the scene changes, I'm on to the next challenge. No time to celebrate or enjoy a victory. I'm sure to some extent this tendency toward negative thinking has served us, but I'd sure love to find a better way to experience life. I'm working on it.

My sister reminded me recently that I've always been like this. When I applied to Harvard Business School, after months of hard work and more months of agonized waiting, a small envelope arrived. I felt an immediate sense of discouragement. Clearly I hadn't gotten in.

Winsome opened the letter. She shouted, "You got in!"

I couldn't believe it. I was ecstatic for, oh, five seconds. And then, as Winsome recounts, my face turned from joy to terror in a flash. My first words were, "How am I going to pay for it?" This was a similar moment. We'd gotten the money. But all I could think was, *How are we going to preserve it?* I saw it as a dwindling asset before we'd spent a penny.

Well, in that case, I was right. No sooner was the money in the bank than it started going out. The first payments were to our attorney, Kiril, for all his work to get us to this stage. Then we had to buy computers (the cheapest available in the Apple Store). I checked the bank account literally every day. It's unclear what sort of miracle I was hoping would occur, but I knew to the dollar, every day (and still do), how much money we had in the bank. I felt like I was watching an old-fashioned hourglass: you flip that thing upside down and the sand slowly flows through. At some point, unless more sand is put in, it will run out. Could we make a success out of Big Think before it was empty?

The reality in most start-ups is that the first round of funding is never enough. To make money, you need money, as the old saying goes. So, less than six months after our first round of funding, the question most immediately on my mind was, where would more capital come from? It was a pretty dodgy economy as we began looking, so VCs were a stretch for us. We weren't a technology play, we were a content/education company and at that time content had become something of a dirty word. (These things are cyclical. As we know, content is once again "queen" as Larry Summers put it for my benefit at an investor lunch in 2014.)

It was evident that wealthy individual investors would be our best path. And these individuals tend to be men—older, white men, to be precise (a situation that is, however, beginning to change today with the rise of women investor networks). It's fair to say that many women I've talked with feel frustrated by how things are, but it doesn't have to be a disadvantage. As a younger, female founder, I've been very successful in raising money in such circumstances.

And given all the disadvantages women face in business, there's no shame in using every asset we have, including dressing to impress. I don't mean "wear something slutty." Investors aren't going to invest just because they like the way you look. But women also have more creative freedom to make an impression with their appearance—not just on the guy sitting across from us, but on our own confidence. When it comes to raising money, an endeavor in which many female founders feel disadvantaged, I believe we have an opportunity to play to our strengths. I'll share more fashion tips in Chapter 6, but for now, by way of an example, let me take you inside one of my pitch meetings during the early years of Big Think.

At this point, the company was no longer just an idea, it was a thing. A real thing. But it was a thing that was fast running out of money, so I needed to make a good impression. The meeting was scheduled over lunch in New York's Theater District. The potential investor was (of course) older, white, and male. I'd been introduced by a friend and was told that this fellow might be interested in what we do. I always dress up for meetings, no matter who. Understanding my audience, I dressed up a little more than usual, in a way that was both noticeably fashionable yet also totally appropriate. A great outfit catches people off guard—it looks well put together, yet surprisingly cool. I wore a layered skirt and my often-complimented, over-the-knee, Stuart Weitzman suede boots. I looked stylish, inviting, yet also like a pro. Confident. That's the key. Study after study confirms that people tend to equate confidence with competence.

> Study after study
> confirms that people tend
> to equate confidence
> with competence.

When it comes to confidence, you don't have to fake it; own it. Women have good reason to be confident. A BCG (Boston Consulting Group) study recently showed that female-run start-ups outperformed male-run start-ups dramatically when it came to giving funders a return on their investment. Despite raising less money than their male counterparts, the female-run companies generated seventy-eight cents in revenue per dollar of investment raised, compared to thirty-one cents generated by the male-run companies.[5] Remember that when you're about to ask for money. And make sure you look good too. Trust me, it helps.

As we sat down to lunch that day, I asked the potential investor what he did, who he was, what he was passionate about. Of course, I'd done my homework and knew the basics before the meeting began, but you learn more from the eye-to-eye conversation. You get to see what really excites the person, and guess what, they get to see what really excites you. That can be a deal closer on both sides. We were at the restaurant for at least two hours—no drinks involved—hell, it was a Monday at lunch! Talking, learning about each other, and sharing stories. By the time we were finished, they were almost setting up for dinner (and the wait staff was about to have family meal—guess who was no longer welcome?). Lunch meetings like this, where it's all about ideas, are often the most meaningful I've had. Many people say the drinks meetings are the most valuable; for me, that's not true at all. It's about creating a situation where investors get a real glimpse of who you are and why they should invest in *you*.

The business idea is key, of course, but it's true that people invest in people. Several weeks later, we got a significant investment.

Fashion aside, here's my number-one tip for making yourself attractive to investors: be truly interested in the person you are meeting or don't bother meeting. The same rule applies for investors whom I follow for colleagues: it's 100 percent advisable to like being around them. If you haven't yet met them and therefore don't know whether you like them, you should at least respect them. In advance of any meeting, do your homework on potential investors. Know things about them beyond the superficial resumé bullet points. If you are asking for money, you sure as shit better know who they are, what they have done, and why they ought to be interested in your venture. You should know as much as possible about what they've already invested in so you can explain why your venture may be complementary to their portfolio. But that's basic. Dig a little deeper than their LinkedIn profile—read up on their passions, their philanthropic pursuits, their life stories. You need to know what turns them on mission-wise. If you don't go prepared, you are wasting precious time. Men (or anyone, for that matter) with resources to invest rightfully expect that you make an effort. Showing up without having done your homework is just wrong. It's disrespectful. You are on the make, and it's protocol to be prepared.

Here are some questions to guide your background research: Why should they be interested in what you do, or what you are seeking to do? What makes them tick, beyond their work? Are they interested in the arts? Theater? Have they given to charities? If so, which ones? Is there a theme to their giving that can help you understand what matters to them? Be ready to investigate. The more you know before you sit down, the better. It will help if you actually have things to talk about beyond the investment. Unless it's a huge acquisition—and perhaps even if it is—people invest in people they like and want to talk with. So be a good conversationalist. I know it's a loaded word, but be charming. Make eye contact. Helping others feel attractive and special—not in a sexual way but in a human way—helps them see you as a more attractive person too. But you have to mean it. Empty flattery won't get you far. Make the effort to authentically find something about your potential investors that you are drawn to, whether it be their smarts, their work, their generosity, or their sense of humor.

If tips like these make you roll your eyes, I understand. Do men have to jump through so many hoops to get funded? No. Do men get judged so intensely on their appearance? No. Too many guys can just show up in a crumpled suit, oozing confidence, and walk out with a check. But look at it this way: guys don't have the opportunity to rock a pair of over-the-knee boots at a business meeting! Women do. Own it. I use everything I've got. I turn my femininity to my advantage. And whatever anyone may think about that, it's served me well in the ongoing (and never-ending) fundraising process.

SAYING "NO" IS ALSO THE JOB OF THE CEO

One of the things I had to do, particularly before we were funded, was make sure we dodged the small army of folks pretending to help the business but actually trying to help themselves. Here's the truth: there are a lot of good people out there, but sometimes shitty people come along and lead you astray. This has happened to us repeatedly. They would take a ridiculous interest in the company and then try to work their way into an equity position for doing next to nothing. It's been up to me to recognize them and put a stop to them. That means to essentially say no to whatever it is they want, no matter how uncomfortable or entangled you are with them. Loyalty to the company above all else.

The first time it happened, I had been introduced by a friend to some supposedly uber-connected guy I'll call Jake, who said he could help get us funded. We met with Jake several times over the course of 2006, but he was never clear what he was after. It seemed he was willing to help because he liked us and the idea. Over the short time he was in our orbit, I kept saying to Peter, "This man is really not doing anything for us and seems to be insinuating that he is in some sort of a partnership role with us." He hadn't brought us any investors, he hadn't booked any experts, he hadn't helped us put together the deck, so what were we doing spending time with him? He felt sort of sleazy, like a smooth talker but not a doer.

Eventually it made me really uncomfortable, and I told Peter I thought we had better either sever ties with Jake or at the very least make his position explicit. At the most, we agreed, he would have a very small stake in Big Think if and only if he actually contributed. We weren't funded at this point, and I'm very grateful we weren't, as I bet he would have pushed way harder had there been money at stake.

In the autumn of 2006, we met Jake on the roof of Soho House, where he was a member. I was nervous. Peter was, too. But I knew I could handle it. When the shit hits the fan, I am often at my most calm. I am somehow able to become singularly focused.

Big Thinkers Say . . .

Big Think expert Emma Seppälä, science director of the Center for Compassion and Altruism Research and Education at Stanford University and author of The Happiness Track, says that tapping into our parasympathetic nervous system in challenging or high-stress moments, rather than relying on 'fight or flight," can be effective.[6] "We know that short-term stress can be great, it can really get you through a deadline and mobilize you. However, if you depend on that day after day after day, you'll find that your body becomes worn out,"[7] she says. She recommends breathing exercises to calm the mind in intense situations.

Jake arrived, and we ordered drinks. He started talking about being a cofounder and partner with us. I took a deep breath and interrupted him.

"Jake, we need to be very clear with you. You are not a cofounder or partner. We may provide some equity to you when we are funded, but there will be very clear parameters around that."

His face grew enraged. Peter, being a people-pleaser by nature and, at this early stage in his career, not liking confrontation, tried to smooth things over with him. Jake began listing all the things he'd done for us, accusing us of being bad, deceitful people. Peter, trying to calm the tense situation, took on an apologetic tone. I didn't back down. Even though it was Jake's club and we were his guests, he put his drink down, stood up, and walked out. My heart was racing. I don't like confrontation either, but had realized the longer the unclarity went on, the more he would try to work his way in.

After he left, Peter and I were both upset, but relieved. The incident taught me a very important lesson. Do not get coerced into business agreements. Also, set very clear expectations about what business relationships are and are not. Define the parameters and do not back down if the person is promising things and not delivering. You need to be as clear as you can. If you are paying people, not everybody gets equity, and if they do, they better have earned it. To deserve equity, a person needs to be bringing to the table something that you can't simply hire. They need to be contributing something exceptional that helps build the company, not just a plug-and-play skill set. Don't let unscrupulous people try to convince you otherwise. Charlatans are like poisonous mosquitoes dressed as butterflies. And it's key to recognize it quickly and root them out. As a leader or founder of a business, saying no is part of your job, even in uncomfortable situations. I've had many such uncomfortable conversations over the years. And I've not always recognized the charlatans right away. We've paid a lot of money to "consultants" who talked a good game and wormed their way in, only to recognize after a few months that, hey, nothing's being accomplished. You can't win them all, but move on as soon as you spot someone taking advantage of you.

"ROOT, HOG, OR DIE"

The early American colonists used to turn their pigs loose in the woods to fend for themselves, hence the common expression "root, hog, or die"—an idiom for self-reliance. Well, that's exactly the feeling we had right after we got funded (and, to be honest, most days since!). We knew that we didn't have a long window of financing, so we had to find clients or sponsors for our content well before we even had a website. Peter and I are master networkers and identified people we could talk to about sales. It was not an easy sell—no website, nothing to show, and needing to get money in the door as soon as possible. But we were persuasive.

Our first sponsor was Pfizer, secured based on relation-ships Peter had within the organization. They would go on to be long-term partners of ours. Next came MSNBC. I'd had a vague interaction with one of the heads of digital adver-tising there. I reached out to fill him in on Big Think and suggested that perhaps we could be partners of MSNBC. We talked for weeks about possible scenarios. Finally, they had a need. GE and SAP wanted to sponsor some expert-driven content, and back then it was unclear even to them what this meant. But we were nimble and could help. Our tiny start-up with very little funding actually became a content creator for MSNBC. That might have seemed like a crazy fantasy, and many entrepreneurs might not even entertain such an idea, but actually it wasn't as unlikely as it sounds. These giant companies get opportunities and sometimes, because they are so big, they are not nimble enough to execute on what they need to do. Smaller companies with greater agility can take advantage of this situation if they just have the courage to step up and offer.

I went to agency meetings for both SAP and GE and man-aged to convince the agencies that we could book exceptional guests and develop content specifically around leadership. Without us, MSNBC would not have been able to deliver. We had to scramble to pull it off, but we did. I assured the agencies we could do it. I told myself, we have to. And we did. The ability to operate in such high-risk situations requires compartmen-talization, and I've become pretty good at it. If I'd focused on all the barriers to achieving the launch, much less delivering two sponsorships with leading experts in a matter of weeks, we wouldn't have made it. One foot in front of the other. What can I do right now? It's that simple.

A NOTE ON VCS

No chapter on fundraising would be complete without a brief discussion of venture capitalists. For us, VC firms have not proven to be a successful source of funding. And the people who work in them are not my favorite human beings. VCs are, by and large, deeply egotistical white men who believe that any company they have or their firm has invested in has succeeded because of them and their incomparable wisdom. That's often not true. They tend to take massive credit where credit is not due. They didn't build the company; they found people who were capable of building it or already had, and invested capital. Yes, capital matters, but it's rarely the ultimate reason for success or failure.

The job of a VC when meeting with entrepreneurs is to find the flaws in what they are doing/have done. And the "older" you are as a start-up (heaven forbid you've become a full-fledged company with not a lot of backing), the less desirable you are. Like Sunset Boulevard. They don't want you to have your close-up—hell, they don't even want to see you! But the truth is, even after being in business for years, you can still find yourself in need of funds. So, not too long ago, Peter and I found ourselves in a VC's office in San Francisco, after having had a few deflating sales meetings in the Bay Area. Why had I even agreed to meet this guy? I should've known better. But I always think there's a chance. Enter this small, blonde-tinted-haired dude. He seemed nice, for a split second, but then, immediately condescending.

"You look tired," he told us. Bitch slap to us both. It was a power play. We had created an incredible company, and yeah, after many years, I'm a little weary. How about you, Mr. (almost always Mr.) VC, try to make payroll and worry about it? How about you try living with being personally liable for the company credit cards, knowing that if you don't make payroll, the employees can sue you? You've never taken a professional risk in your life, and you believe that being a VC, with somebody else's money behind you, makes you a big, swinging dick. Think again, man. You are no risk-taker. You are banking on the risks others take, and telling them that they don't even deserve what they are making. The oft-heard line, told in different ways, is that VCs want their entrepreneurs to be hungry. It makes them desperate to achieve. I'll tell you what it's done to me: it has made me anxious as fuck. Have I performed? Hell, yeah. Do I have respect for VCs? Not really. Unless they have sweated it out themselves, and, as crass as it sounds, paid their fucking dues.

Arrogant VCs aside, we've had the privilege of receiving investments from many outstanding individuals over the years. Our investors are some of the people I respect the most, and I'm honored (and rather intimidated) that they've placed their trust, and their money, in me and in Big Think. Raising money is never easy, but it comes with an unexpected benefit, I've discovered—the opportunity to meet lifelong friends, advisors, and mentors.

REFLECTIONS

- Confidence matters. Figure out what makes you extraordinary and capitalize on it.

- Demonstrate sincere interest. Being truly interested in someone else will make that person more interested in you.

- You don't always need to know how to do things; you need to know how to ask people to do things for you.

- Learn to say no.

- Ambiguity is the enemy. Set clear expectations of whatever deal or relationship you are entering into.

CHAPTER 3

GROW A PAIR

....

What It (Really) Takes to Get a Business Off the Ground

Do you actually need a pair to be an entrepreneur? Hell no, but it's a reference we all get. To my mind, it means get some qualities that traditionally tend to be associated with men or masculinity—things like strength, resilience, guts, fearlessness. Of course, these qualities are absolutely not unique to those with testicles. Plus, as several comedians have pointed out, it's ironic that we should choose the most tender and vulnerable part of the male anatomy to represent them! There are parts of the female anatomy that might be much more appropriate candidates. Nevertheless, it strikes me that much of the language of risk-taking—which is what being an entrepreneur is all about—has a decidedly masculine tone. For example, we say "man up" when we want someone to be courageous. And we call someone who is weak or fearful a "pussy."

Traditionally feminine qualities may not feature prominently in the lexicon of risk-taking, but that doesn't mean women aren't every bit as capable of doing it. Hell, it took just as much courage for me to start Big Think as any man, and likely more. It also took tenacity, resilience, and most important of all, action. You as an entrepreneur (and maybe CEO) need to get shit done, not merely *think* about getting shit done. Will you fail a lot? Yes, but you need to get going and accomplishing. Reports and plans aren't going to help much in the early stages. Action is what matters. So, let's grab those balls and get going.

TURNING FEAR TO AN ADVANTAGE

Entrepreneurs, whether their endeavor turns out to be successful long term or not, need to be able to confront and manage fear. Managing the fear of failure and also anxiety (topics I'll return to in more depth in Chapter 9) have been critical skills for me to learn. I still struggle with them today, after more than a decade in business, but at the outset of a venture they can be particularly acute. Here are some strategies that worked for me:

- Wherever you go, introduce yourself as an entrepreneur in the present tense.

- Tell people you meet about what you are building.
- Turn to your advantage the fear of failing to execute by moving through it and doing.

Executing, for me, has been helpful in managing fear. I'm focusing on what I'm doing, so I do not have my focus on fear. It's sitting around and worrying about what needs to be done, rather than actually doing it, that drives fear into me. This strategy doesn't mean the feeling will go away (sorry!), but it does mean you will move through it.

Big Thinkers Say . . .

Amy Cuddy, social psychologist and associate professor of Business Administration at Harvard Business School, has taught about presence on Big Think and some of her lessons are invaluable for women who want to start their own ventures.[1] The critical lesson is to access your core values using personal power, or power over self. "The way to a healthy and happy life is not to be focused on winning. It's to be focused on having real meaningful authentic interactions and knowing that you did what you could and that you can't control everything the other person does or what they think of you,"[2] she says.

Additionally, Cuddy talks about harnessing the tools you already possess, like your *knowledge, skills, and personality.* Personal power is infinite—everyone can be personally powerful. And personal power as an entrepreneur is action. The goal is to build or create something and the personal power required to do that is action. It also requires self-belief. For me, it was about believing I would raise money. I would start this business no matter what. I would figure out how to support myself. Whatever it took, I would do.

Here's the thing: I don't know if the entrepreneurial drive is nature or nurture. Am I a natural-born entrepreneur? I will say that I've always had a drive to not tolerate the status quo. When people tell me I can't do things, I say, fuck it, I'll show you I can. Personal power, again! When I was in my mid-twenties and working for a Toronto consulting firm, I had this notion that I wanted to run a movie studio. (No, I wasn't one of those entitled young people who wanted to leap ahead before paying my dues; I just wanted to pay my dues *faster*.) I didn't even know what running a studio meant, but I flew out to Los Angeles to check it out. My sister Winsome was living there at the time, working to be an actress. I knew nobody else in town, but after spending a few days there, I made my decision: I was going to move to LA and enter the entertainment world. I didn't give myself a backup plan—I just gave my notice, packed my things, and moved. I had no job, no money, and just a place to sleep on my sister's apartment floor in a dodgy part of LA. Apparently, we had major drug dealers living in our building as well as an undercover cop.

Within days, I hustled and got a job as an unpaid intern, while waiting tables at night. I was told at the internship (and by pretty much anybody in the business) that there was a very clear timeline for advancing in Hollywood and no way around it. Six to twelve months as an intern, minimum, then you move to the mailroom for a year or more, then you become an assistant for years, eventually becoming a more senior assistant before moving on to junior executive or agent. Hell no.

I didn't have the time, patience, or money for this schedule. "I will be an assistant in under a year," I told people. They laughed. But I gave myself a deadline and, you know what? I made it. My internship lasted two months, then I moved to a mailroom job for a few months before going to work at Summit Entertainment for Modi Wiczyk—all in less than a year. Heck, it's so long ago I can't remember, but it may have been less than six months. It turned out Modi had also bucked the trend and didn't "wait" for the normal trajectory—he made it happen himself. I had lucked out finding a role model and an early coach.

This is how I learned the importance of setting a deadline and a clear target for anything you really want to achieve in your life, professionally at least. I also learned the importance of finding and working with people you admire who are following the career you want to have. If you identify them and make it clear they are mentors to you, they will be invested in you. I've always found mentors who are outside the norm, because I want to be outside the norm. I don't want to play by the rules, and I don't.

CEO, MAKEUP ARTIST, GOFER: YOUR JOB IS WHATEVER NEEDS DOING

Back to those balls. After I quit my day job, Peter and I looked at each other and asked, *What now?* Before we could launch our website, we needed content. And there was no way that big-name experts were going to come knocking on our door when we didn't even have a website. So we decided to go to them. Where were the kind of people we wanted to feature? Well, we knew a bunch of them were at Harvard. So, in the spring of 2007, we packed up all our newly purchased camera equipment and headed to Cambridge. Through total scrappiness and chutzpah, we managed to line up interviews with cognitive psychologist and popular science author Steven Pinker, legal scholar Alan Dershowitz, business thinker Clayton Christensen, and economist Michael Porter, among others. We managed to get them because we strongly believed in the mission of Big Think and conveyed it to them in a compelling way. I've learned that, at least for me, truly believing in what I do and expressing that succinctly and compellingly has proven essential to convincing others to participate.

We were pretty chill during the set up for the first interviews, which were to be conducted on the HBS campus, across the river from Harvard College. We'd given ourselves a lot of time to ensure a seamless experience for the guest. I'd stayed up late preparing, as I would be conducting the interviews. I felt a faint buzz of nervousness, but I knew I was ready. This was it. We were really doing this. Everything was set up, and in a few minutes our first expert would arrive: Michael Porter.

Then, disaster struck. Our head of production realized that the battery on the mic was dead. And we didn't have another one. Crap! What were we to do? The nearest electronics store was across the river: a ten-minute walk on a good day. I leaped up and began to run, in my high-heeled boots. That's what you do when you have things on the line—anything it goddamn takes. No thinking, just doing. Hesitation is the enemy. It was a blazing hot day and by the time I made it back with the battery I was blistered and soaked in sweat.

Michael had arrived, so I introduced myself: "Thank you so much for being here. I'm Victoria, CEO of Big Think." Then I showed him to the makeup chair. "I'll also be your makeup artist today." Trying not to drip sweat on him, I began applying base and powder. No, I'd never done that before, but, hey, someone had to do it. I pulled myself together, and the interview was under way. Within minutes I had gone from being a gofer on a critical, albeit small, mission to sitting in front of one of the smartest minds on the planet.

As Michael started to speak, blisters and batteries were instantly forgotten. This was why we were working our asses off to build the company: because brilliant people like him had wisdom to share and we could help more people have access to it. Hell, I could feel myself getting smarter as I listened, and did my best to ask my questions. It was like a shot in the arm of purpose and passion, a timely reminder of our mission and the value we could bring to the world.

When you're getting a start-up off the ground, you do whatever you have to do, and wear whatever hat needs wearing. *CEO* has a nice ring to it, but if the company needs a gofer to run for batteries, you'd better be in good shape (also, carry sneakers). For our early interviews, Peter and I booked, prepped, powdered, interviewed, produced, and schlepped. We didn't let anything—major or minor—derail us. That's what it takes to get a new venture started. If an entrepreneur needs to grow a pair of anything, perhaps it should be an extra pair of arms.

When you're getting a start-up off the ground, you do whatever you have to do, and wear whatever hat needs wearing.

We got our first batch of interviews recorded. Next step? Finding a place to work. So, in yet another unexpected role, I temporarily became a real estate agent. Who else was going to find us an office without charging a broker's fee? My shitty little, mouse-infested studio apartment was not exactly calling our name, although we seriously considered it. Eventually, we found an architect's office on Broadway where we could rent a desk. Peter and I sat back to back—the first of many times we have literally almost sat on top of each other.

Every morning, we'd show up and ask ourselves, okay, so what do we need to achieve today? Blank slate or blue skies, as people like to say. In some ways it was invigorating; in some ways it was paralyzing.

DO SOMETHING EVERY DAY

Getting a business off the ground is overwhelming. It isn't always clear precisely what you should be doing on a daily basis, much less moment to moment. Here's my approach: *it doesn't matter where you start—just start!* Don't become paralyzed by the enormous list of tasks ahead of you. Do something every day to further your objective. Every step matters. It doesn't have to be a great big task, like writing a business plan. In fact, making the tasks too big is a surefire way of not doing them. It should be clear, manageable steps, like "I will call X person." or "I will set up a company Twitter profile," or "I will open a bank account." The little things matter and add up and must be done to move forward. There are so many seemingly trivial tasks that go into starting and running a business that had never occurred to me until it was my job to do them. And along the way, they just keep coming up. Make each task realistic, and do not let yourself off the hook until you have done it. Motivational speaker and bestselling author Jack Canfield tells the story of how, back when his first book came out, he literally sat down with a pile of yellow sticky notes, and on each note he wrote one thing he could do to promote his book. Then he stuck them on his office wall—a thousand of them. And every day, his commitment was to take down one sticky note and complete the task. That's a great strategy for a start-up.

One of the first tasks on our metaphorical sticky notes was getting a URL. We knew the company name we wanted: the Big Think. We incorporated. But we didn't have a URL. We were a website company, but we had nowhere to build a website. Our preferred URL—thebigthink.com—was owned by a man in Australia. I reached out repeatedly but got no response. We really wanted *the* in front of Big Think. But sometimes you need to just *move* and settle for what you can get.

Big Thinkers Say . . .

Entrepreneur Tim Ferriss says in his Big Think interview that procrastination is the enemy.[3] Get going and, even if it seems like you're lowering your standards, move ahead. "There are many tools in the toolkit," he says, "but keep it small, keep it defined, rig it so you can win and when in doubt figure out a way to create a loss or shame if you don't actually tackle your task and achieve some type of measurable goal by a specific point in time."[4]

The other thing Ferriss teaches is that we can become demoralized by setting our standards too high and locking

> onto a specific outcome that can prevent us from com-
> pleting what we need to get done. What's that line—the
> perfect is the enemy of the good?

We thought *The Big Think* was perfection. We were hung up on it, but it wasn't available, and what good was an internet company without a URL? Reluctantly, we decided to look for alternatives. We discovered that bigthink.com was owned by South Korean URL squatters. After contacting the owner, a negotiation ensued. I had anticipated some cost but not a lot—like a token $500. But no. The price started out at $100,000 with no wiggle room. After weeks of back and forth, I successfully negotiated it down (over email) to $35,000. Another (to my mind) huge expense, and yet another hat. Now I was real estate agent, negotiator with South Korean URL hoarders, and CEO. The real lesson in the experience was this: sometimes, not getting what you want is a blessing. Bigthink.com was actually a much better URL and a better brand for our company. Thank goodness! Had we held out for what we thought was perfection, we would have ended up with a second-rate brand. This was one of many instances in which not getting what we wanted led us to something much better

Another example? In the early days, we thought that putting our experts directly in touch with our audience would be compelling, so we wanted to build from scratch the ability to do remote web interviews from our webcam and also allow our audience to upload them. Guess what? Technology changes so fast: with open-source developing and on the rise, it made no sense for us to build anything from scratch on the tech side of things. We invested a ton of money in something that ended up having a really bad functionality. We never even used it. We could have stopped there, panicked, and stuck our heads in the sand. It was quite a setback. But the thing is, this was actually good for us. It forced us to double down on our own production process, to realize that we would be creating *all* the content and that we also needed to expand into written content to have sufficient daily content to attract an audience. We also realized (duh) that SEO (search engine optimization), especially at that time, was driven mostly by written content and if we only had video on our site we would have severely bad SEO.

These kinds of setbacks can feel insurmountable. We'd spent a ton of the money we initially raised on a very fancy website and platform that ended up not providing us value. The sunk cost really weighed on us. Looking back now, though, I see it as a blessing. Had the interview platform succeeded, we would have been just another user-generated content provider. We would have been unlikely to continue to attract top experts if they were featured alongside user-generated content, the brand that we built over the previous twelve-plus years would be totally different and nowhere near the caliber of who we are today.

So, my advice? Embrace the failures. These "restarts" will happen regularly. Understand that things didn't work out for a reason, and take time to reflect with your team, advisors, customers, audience—anybody who will give you feedback—on why it failed and why not working could actually be a plus. It likely won't occur to you overnight, but it will come and once it does there is an opportunity to turn your attention to things that will truly add value. In this instance, for us, it was honing our production and editorial processes and furthering our brand and product.

There are countless examples of things that didn't work out for us and then turned out to be blessings. Yes, it's also true that sometimes things not working out just plain sucked—losing a client, not getting a major contract, and so on. But again, there is a light here—what can you learn from this? What could you have done better? How will you make sure it doesn't happen again? In these moments, where we can, we've implemented processes to prevent these situations, whether it's been building a client success team to prevent churn and serve customers better or instituting weekly meetings to go over outstanding pitches and losses.

YOU DO YOU. GET OTHERS TO DO THE REST

Office? Check (kind of). URL? Check. What next? Accountant. I hadn't considered that we'd need someone to actually manage our finances and pay bills. For the first month or so, it was me. This is not my forte. I am a doer, but I am not methodical. At. All. As Peter will attest, my apartment is always impeccable but my work desk is always a mess. I quickly realized I needed to focus on doing the things that would move us forward, and outsource everything else to the extent I could. I asked around, and with great luck, my brother-in-law suggested an accountant he'd worked with for his start-up, Roy Cupples. Roy has been Big Think's longest freelance employee and is someone I trust implicitly. But to have Roy work with us I had to switch back to real estate agent. We needed another desk in the architecture firm's space, as we couldn't share our inappropriately small workspace with a professional. So, I got us another desk.

These things seem trivial, and yet, they actually matter! When our first two full-time employees, Brett and Eddie, came on board, they shared that desk space, unless Roy was in the office and then one of them floated. Or Peter and I squeezed in even tighter and gave them part of our desk space. Yes, and to get Brett and Eddie, I became head of HR for Big Think—negotiated their salaries, benefits, and equity. Another role.

So, with a tiny team in place and an actual URL, it was time to get down to actually creating our product. We'd gotten a few interviews on our trip to Boston, but we needed to start creating studio interviews. We knew that we wanted the Big Think brand to be stand-alone, so we decided it was best to have no personality behind the camera—not even Peter or me. Neither of us was keen to become another Mr. Snider anyway. But how to shoot, without an on-air interviewer? Time to seek more advice from folks who might know.

My friend Kate Milliken, who I'd brought on to work on a freelance project with Snider years earlier, came to mind. Kate had been an on-air personality for the likes of monster truck shows and had recently started her own company, Videode, to create personal videos for people and their families. She suggested I speak with a fellow named Manny Kivowitz, and it was Manny who introduced us to the Errol Morris Interrotron way of shooting. This format means that the person being interviewed is looking directly into the camera because the interviewer's face is being mirrored and looking directly at the subject. Unlike a lot of interviews where interviewees are looking off to the side, they are seemingly making eye contact with the viewer. It's very effective for a personal interviewing style, and it makes interviewees comfortable. They really feel they are having a conversation with the person interviewing them. We paid Manny a consulting fee and he went to B&H (a massive photo and video store in New York) with our new head of production, Eddie Vidales, to purchase equipment. Manny was also going to train Eddie how to shoot with the new equipment. In a start-up, every member has to learn new things and go way beyond his or her comfort zone—it's not just the founders.

Equipment? Check. Lightweight team? Check. Time to start booking our first few studio interviews. In fact, we used Manny's studio for the first few as we did not yet have our own. Now, my ever-expanding list of roles included booker, producer, and location scout. And I was about to become interviewer as well. This was a new experience for me. I'd certainly prepared Snider for interviews, but besides our initial Boston session, I'd never actually done them myself. My first two subjects were the singer Moby, whom I'd met through a mutual friend, and the Columbia professor Robert Thurman on Buddhism. It's an interesting transition to suddenly be responsible for getting the content from the interviewee, and it can be hard, especially if the person is not a big talker.

The interview with Thurman was a particularly interesting foray into my new job. Although I should have known, given the research and preparation I'd done for the interview, I didn't realize that he had a prosthetic eye, due to an accident. I was already nervous about interrogating such a formidable mind. When the interview began and only one eye was blinking, while the other stayed totally trained on me, it kind of freaked me out. But he was so inspiring and warm and brilliant that I soon became totally absorbed in his wisdom and knowledge and getting the best content I could for Big Think. You certainly couldn't tell from the interview that anything was amiss as the man is a total pro and passionate about teaching.

Were my first efforts seamless? No. Like everything, interviewing takes practice. My first few attempts were either way shorter or way longer than they should have been, as I was not comfortable in the interviewer's chair. In some cases, I whipped through the questions, just wanting to get as much as I could from the person before they had to leave, not realizing that I really should have been following up on some of the questions to get richer material. In other cases, I let the guest drone on, focusing on one subject for far too long, and not get all that we came to get. I got better as I went along, and actually became pretty good. Over the years, I have trained others to do it, as my role morphed primarily into the business side of things. I love knowledge and content creation. One of the main reasons I started Big Think was precisely because of that. But, over time I did less of it because my role necessarily changed. Every entrepreneur's role will change over the lifetime of the company. At first, your priority is just to keep the business afloat; later, hopefully, it's to drive growth.

EVERYONE NEEDS A COACH. IT'S YOUR JOB TO FIND ONE

I have no doubt that I would not be where I am today without the help of many coaches, mentors, and advisors I've been lucky enough to have. Mentors aren't just for the early part of your journey—they're critical at every stage. I've been blessed to have exceptional ones throughout my career. Find the right people and make yourself accountable to them. Ask if you can check in with them regularly so they can hold you to your objectives. You certainly won't want to let them down. These people don't have to be investors (though oftentimes they will become them).

Good mentors not only help you navigate, they help you get ahead and give you a kick in the ass to press you to achieve.

They don't even have to know that they are a mentor to you—just by creating a relationship in which you tell them what you are doing and what you intend to achieve, you can make them a de facto mentor because you'll feel the pressure to live up to the expectations you set.

For women entrepreneurs, having a mentor can be particularly effective. We always hear that women are more relationship-oriented than men and may have more of a tendency to people-please. Well, let's use that! I certainly have. And be sure to choose someone who has high expectations of you. It's been my observation that, in general, male entrepreneurs are seen as more likely to succeed (at least in their own minds and so maybe in the minds of their mentors) and are therefore held to higher standards than the seemingly meeker, less aggressive female entrepreneur. To me, that's based on false assumptions, and it gives women too much room to fail. What's kept me in absolute check is that I've surrounded myself with mentors who won't take one bite of bullshit. Not even a sniff of it. Harsh in the moment, powerful and super helpful in the long term. I've always had a penchant for identifying alpha males, professionally, and learning from them. I'm not cocky, but I'm super direct, and this seems to endear me to these men. They like that I'm to the point and pull no punches. I say what I think. And, you better believe, they do the same. And then some. It helps drive me to get things done. Remember, getting shit done is your job as the entrepreneur.

We all need different sorts of mentors, so identify what "genre" suits you best. For me, initially (I've softened some), the tougher they were, the better. I don't want just a cheerleader, I want someone who will take me to task, who will question what I am doing and give me honest, sometimes harsh, feedback and ask me to act on it. The mentor "type" I gravitate toward will be different than yours. Mine stemmed from having an alpha father—he was blunt, no-bullshit, saw the excellence in others, strove to bring it out of them, and required performance. At least initially, I was a little in awe of and intimidated by the mentors I chose. For me, that intimidation was actually motivating.

I've had female mentors and coaches, too, but in the start-up world, there are a hell of a lot more men. If you can find female mentors, in addition to male mentors, whether you're male or female, that's a precious thing. One woman I've learned from the most is Carla Newman. Carla is a serial entrepreneur who has sold two businesses and is on to her third. I met her through her father, Hal, who was introduced to me as a potential investor. Hal brought Carla in to vet us, and they ended up becoming investors. Carla eventually even became a Big Think board member. She's been instrumental in helping me and the company through critical patches. What's been especially useful, with Carla, is that she understands the uniqueness of being a female entrepreneur in a man's world. She's been in similar situations as me: often the only woman in the room, and often dealing with enormous egos.

I watch her and observe how she rarely gets flustered and treats it like a "fun" game. She's mentored me to not sweat the small stuff, to trust that things *will* work out, one way or another. Through her, I've learned about optimism in ways I wouldn't have expected. I'm a get-it-done kind of gal—planning for success but focused on failure. She's the opposite—always, or at least monthly, focusing on what can go right. I'm generally an optimist in a broad sense, but can get caught up in the depression and failures of the moment and not see the progress being made. Not Carla—she's a constant voice of encouragement and support. When the chips are down, she's there even more, rolling up her sleeves and leading by example. Over the last five years, she's come to be one of the people I most respect. Over and over, we've been on the brink of going out of business—like most start-ups—and she got in the trenches and helped me sort through how to move forward, with no judgment. She even personally invested when things looked grim—a tangible sign of her belief in me and the company. This is the sort of person you want around, male or female.

Big Thinkers Say . . .

You need mentors at every stage of life and profession. You always need someone to tell you the real truth about how you are doing and how you are interacting with others. It's critical. Get over yourself and get help. Robert Kaplan, now head of the Dallas Fed and former vice chairman of Goldman Sachs, speaks to this in his Big Think Edge masterclass, "The Leadership Challenge." "The most sig-nificant reason that I see that leaders fail," he declares, "is not because they're not smart enough or they don't have the skills; it's that they are not open to learning and they are isolated."[5] When leaders become isolated, they stop getting critical feedback. "You don't have that many people above you," he explains. "Maybe you don't have anyone above you. Almost everyone is below you. So therefore many of the decisions you're rum nating over affect all these people below you. And you feel like, 'Boy, I'd love to talk to them about it, but I don't think I can. You know, it involves them. I think it may not be appropriate. Yet there's no one above me. If I don't go out and take proactive steps could get very isolated where no one is giving me advice.'"[6]

That's when people make bad mistakes—ones you can't come back from. They are not fully informed, and so they think they are doing a great job and no one is making them aware of, or seeing real trouble spots. Leaders need coaching as much if not more than those not in leadership positions, Kaplan says. And they need to ask for it. Other-wise, if they surround themselves with yes men, they will truly run the risk of not seeing critical issues.

After more than a decade in business, I value my mentors more than ever. I have several, and one of the most important is Larry Summers. Larry is much more than his jaw-dropping resumé and brilliant mind; he's also my friend. People who are really rooting for you are the best mentors, as tough as they can be. With Larry, he pulls no punches, he's straight up, and he's in it for the long haul. He invested in Big Think at the start, and most important, he invested in me and Peter.

You won't always know whom to choose as a mentor or coach but if they are giving you honest and critical feedback, it's a good start. Pick people who have characteristics that you do not. For instance, I'm anxiety ridden, so having mentors who are confident and positive is useful for me. They help me see situations from a different perspective and open my mind to possibilities.

Ask directly for help. You want to achieve things, and your mentors can only help if they know you need it. Ask. Lay out the challenge or situation and be clear what it is you would like from them. Being vague or sheepish will not get you results.

RESILIENCE IS CRITICAL

Resilience is key to being an entrepreneur. You will be bitch-slapped down—whether you are a woman or a man. You need to keep believing in yourself and your idea when no one else does. Time and again over the years, I've been belittled, as has Big Think, by various people—especially venture capitalists. Bottom line: you need to learn to recognize who respects and admires what you do and avoid those who don't. Never allow yourself to be belittled by someone who doesn't have the same values as you or your organization. Some people will never believe in you and will in fact hold you back by their negativity about you or your idea or even existing business. Don't let them have that power. Keep going.

Being a female entrepreneur will present you with a unique set of circumstances. While "grow a pair" may be viewed as odd advice, it shows you exactly what you are up against. Like it or not, you're in a still-male-dominated world where the traits associated with success are also generally associated with being male. Prove that to be wrong. Make them yours. But also, take advantage of all the ways in which you're different. First, focus on the basics. If you set high expectations, tell others about them, work on things every day, be willing to wear whatever hat needs wearing, and learn to be resilient in the face of discouraging people and events. You can make it. But you'll only get a chance to make it if you start today. So do it.

REFLECTIONS

- Turn fear and shame to your advantage: tell people what you are going to do, and you will be more likely to do t.

- Just start: the hardest thing to do is take the first step. Do it now.

- Get a coach or mentor. Find someone who will hold you accountable to progress and timeline.

- Be resilient. You will have major setbacks. Know they are coming and don't let them stop you.

CHAPTER 4

GET PERSONAL

Working with People You Like,
and Saying Goodbye (Fast)
to Those You Don't

I often dreamed about starting my own business and being my
own boss. But never once did those imaginary scenarios include
having to sit down with an employee and tell him his smelly feet
were disrupting the office. Yet this, and many other awkward
human encounters, became part of my job once Big Think was
up and running. Running a company means hiring, managing,
and sometimes firing people. As obvious as this sounds, it's not
something every start-up founder anticipates or is prepared for.

Finding exceptional people to work with is very, very
hard—and how you handle it can make or break your start-up.

Managing them is an entirely different and huge challenge. I've learned a lot about hiring and firing, delegating, and dealing with all kinds of weird and wacky personnel issues over the last decade. In the end, the people you work with will become a big part of your day-to-day life. You may well spend more time with them than you spend with your own family. So there's no sense in hiring people you don't like, or keeping people on if they're not a good fit. The old adage is true: hire slowly, fire fast.

> ## Finding exceptional people to work with is very, very hard—and how you handle it can make or break your start-up. Managing them is an entirely different and huge challenge.

One of the biggest mistakes I've made is not getting rid of toxic people quickly enough. And also, hiring people when I had even an inkling they may not work out. I think it is true that you're more likely to be successful if you're having fun—and even if you fail, at least you'll have enjoyed the company and the people along the way.

KNOW WHAT YOU ARE ACTUALLY HIRING FOR

In a start-up environment where you are always moving, resources are scarce and you need to execute quickly. Hiring slowly and firing fast can be challenging. It's not always realistic but keeping that principle in mind may save you some heartache down the line. It's also a huge help if you ensure you know exactly what you are hiring for at the early stages of the game. You need people who are willing to roll up their sleeves and get stuff done, rather than create PowerPoints about what "others" might do. My advice: don't hire super-analytical people when you're just getting off the ground. In fact, unless you're hiring for an analyst's job, I'd say it's a good rule even when you've been in business for years

I've made that mistake—a lot. I've hired based purely on past experience and how well the person could talk about the challenges we were facing. I've been wooed by what they said they could do, rather than what they actually did, and hung on to people based on the same principle. I should have recognized earlier that we needed people who could actually get shit done and not just talk about it. For instance, at one point we spent a good deal of money on a sales consultant who had built successful sales teams at various companies and had excellent stats about what he'd achieved. I totally believed his pitch. It turned out, however, that he did not want to do any actual selling himself. He came in and presented ways we should reform our sales pitch processes, but did not actually *sell* anything—which is what we needed. I mean, it's a cliché, but I should have asked to see his hands. If you don't see any callouses, ask: What exactly have you sold and what will you sell for us? This guy hung around (because I believed the hype) for far too long.

At Big Think, we say we want thinkers (the experts) and doers (the team). Our experts are our real thinkers, the people our audience wants to learn from. Our team needs to actually make the business run. One of the key personality traits needed to get the job done is integrity. You can smell and feel integrity, as clearly as I could smell the aforementioned team member's feet. I look for people who are not afraid to speak hard truths. For instance, in the hiring process I like to see if they are no-bullshit people. Complimenting me or the company is fine to a certain degree, but I want to know what the person thinks is crap about the company. Things they've noticed that could be improved easily and that actually annoy them. I mean, they can't know about the team, but they sure better know about the product and have familiarized themselves with it.

I think a first sign of integrity is showing up to an interview with clear ideas of what is working and what could be improved upon and how they'd do it. Integrity can also be (somewhat) identified by asking folks what they've done professionally in their past that they felt called their integrity into question and what they did about it. We've all been confronted by iffy scenarios—sometimes there's a clear ethical path forward, and sometimes it's in the margins. I like to hear about situations like this that our potential hires have confronted. There isn't a "right" answer. Even if they realized post facto that what they did compromised their integrity, that's okay—as long as they learned from it. I also appreciate when people fess up to clear errors of judgment professionally—whether it be interactions with coworkers, clients, or others. We have all done something that makes us cringe. Some people have even been fired for such errors. Those with integrity acknowledge their missteps and grow from them. People who present themselves as the "perfect" candidate, I just don't buy.

Make it your rule that if you get one bad or even questionable feeling about the integrity of a person, even a freelancer, do not hire the person. This isn't about their qualifications, their resumé, or their outward persona—it's about who they *are*. The same goes for someone who's already on your team. If you feel you made a mistake and the person's integrity is not there, let them go. That may sound harsh, but I'll tell you this: 100 percent of the times I have not trusted my gut about someone's integrity, the person has turned out to be wrong for the company. A man once told me that a woman's gift is her intuition, so let's make use of it! Mine is fairly well developed by now, and I've come to trust it. When I have failed to listen to my gut, it has caused me personal distress and burdened the company with toxic individuals. It is true—one bad apple can spoil the lot.

I've also hired exceptional people and have formed wonderful long-term relationships. There is nothing like being in the trenches together to get to know someone's qualities. I've lucked out in bringing on board super-talented people who have stayed with us for years, and some who have been short-term employees but have made outsized contributions. We are a scrappy company and so a lot of the people we have hired have been junior and inexperienced. I have found that this matters far less than their dedication to improving the organization and themselves and moving the mission forward. And junior hires are usually self-starters, constantly looking for new challenges. Our head of instructional design, Elizabeth Rodd, for example, took on the challenge of creating an entirely new framework of content for the company to bring in a new revenue stream. She hired and managed people and set up processes that did not exist before, without guidance or real oversight. She has been with the organization for almost a decade and continues to contribute massively, every day. And guess what? She takes it personally. People who take the work that the organization does as a reflection on themselves are people you want around.

Hiring and firing aside, it's important to ensure the best talent stays with you. Treat them well. Align your hiring with what motivates those people and make sure it is also what is motivating the company. People already in the company want to bring on new colleagues who get the culture and the mission and want to be a part of it. Of course, new hires can suggest and instill new ways of thinking and doing (and we hope they will), but they have to want to be a member of the existing team.

While your company is still small (fewer than twenty people) it's a good idea to have everybody in the organization meet a candidate before you hire anyone. Ask everybody for their opinions and you will learn a lot. In a bigger organization, it may be more practical to select a diverse group of people, from senior leaders to junior staff, to participate in the interview process. It's also important to tell people not to discuss their opinions until everybody has met the candidate, so they don't influence one another. Get candid feedback, but still trust your gut if everybody loves the person and you don't. This process is slow but efficient.

RECOGNIZE CONFIRMATION BIAS

There's a tendency for us to see what we expect to see. This can be really problematic in hiring. Daniel Kahneman—a Big Think expert who won the 2002 Nobel Prize in Economic Sciences for his work on the psychology of judgment, decision-making, and behavioral economics—identified cognitive bias in a 1974 paper with Amos Tversky.[1] A cognitive bias is a kind of mental shortcut or bad habit that humans fall into, which often impacts their choices and judgments. One common cognitive bias is confirmation bias, which is the all-too-common tendency to overvalue evidence that confirms one's existing beliefs and undervalue evidence that contradicts those beliefs. What does that mean for hiring? For me, at least, it's meant that I've likely missed out on great people and hired the wrong ones.

In the early years of Big Think, I was fooled by what was on candidates' resumés—in particular, by where they went to school. If they attended an Ivy League or other notable college, I'd already pegged them as hardworking, talented, and a likely good fit for our "smarter, faster" culture at Big Think. Conversely, if I didn't recognize the college, I often didn't even invite them in for an interview, despite very interesting and impressive achievements on their resumé. Oftentimes, these people had a much humbler background, where they had to be scrappy and innovative to get ahead, likely making them the sort of person who would be a great fit in our company. And I missed that because I couldn't see past my own bias. Instead, we hired at least two Ivy League graduates who were far less hard-working and thoughtful than the rest of the staff. Had I accurately observed them in interviews, I feel I would have seen this.

Big Thinkers Say . . .

After several bad hires based on my biases, I finally began to question my thinking and ask, what are we trying to achieve here? And why am I expecting to see what I expect to see? International Poker Champion Liv Boeree has some great tips on bias. "The most damaging bias which can come up in poker and I think very often in life is what's known as confirmation bias," she says. "That's when you have a pre-existing want to believe something, a desire for something to be true, and you will overvalue evidence that confirms that belief and disvalue evidence that disproves it."[2] When she's playing poker, she applies these strategies, which she shared in her Big Think interview[3]:

First, evaluate your thought process. Ask: Am I looking for signs that prove what I want to believe? Am I dismissing signs that disprove what I want to believe? Then, search for contrary evidence that challenges your intuition. This will give you a more accurate perspective.

LESSONS IN DEALING WITH HIGH-CONFLICT PEOPLE

"Liquid Nitrogen C*nt."

That was certainly the most original insult I'd ever received! Actually, I was not supposed to receive it at all, but one of my staff, who clearly was not my biggest fan, emailed the rest of the team describing me as such. On her Big Think company email. I'd had inklings for weeks that this lady didn't like me, but I had not realized the extent of her disrespect and insubordination.

"Lucy" was one of the aforementioned Ivy Leaguers. Smart, sassy, pushy, and, as we would later find out, entitled, disrespectful, and manipulative. Lucy was an early hire at Big Think, joining Peter, myself, Eddie, and Brett. She was to focus on editorial. We'd been told she was a great writer, and she was friends with Peter's friend from Harvard, who was also a writer. Peter met her first and liked her—plus, since he really trusted his friend, he was already somewhat committed to her. I was excited to meet her. She was young, attractive, and seemingly super confident. Even brash. We sat down at a coffee shop and started talking. I could tell she was smart and talented, but something about her immediately rubbed me the wrong way. Her energy, her aura, I don't know what it was. At that moment, my intuition was telling me that she and I would clash, but I tried to ignore it. I didn't want to seem competitive, like one of those women who can't handle having other smart, powerful women around. I was impressed by her intelligence and her education, and I could tell that she was hungry to make an impression and impact the world with her work. All good things.

What I should have also taken on board was that she was conceited, with a sense of entitlement and grandiosity. Rather than trusting my instincts, I overrode them. I told Peter that I had some personal reservations; however, I wanted the best talent for Big Think and was willing to put my personal feelings aside. Wrong! This was a person I'd have to work with every day in a small space. Not worth it.

On Lucy's first day in the office, I decided to sit beside her. I figured if I could get to know her personally, we might hit it off. Here's the thing, though: if you are worried about hitting it off with someone from the get-go, ideally, that person shouldn't be in your environment. In my position as CEO and cofounder, I didn't have to make the decision to hire her—I had a choice. That's not always true when dealing with clients and partners, but in this case, it was.

My fears about Lucy were borne out. She grudgingly fulfilled some tasks she didn't deem important (to her) as if she were doing us a favor, and although she was talented and good at what she did, she had a snarky demeanor much of the time. She also seemed to have a keen desire to talk smack about anybody and everything. It got worse and worse, and yet I kept my mouth shut. We were a small, close-knit team, and I wanted us to succeed.

From the start, clearly she had issues with me. It's said that there are certain women who do not like working for women. I cannot be sure, but it strikes me that she had queen bee syndrome, meaning she liked to be the alpha female in the room. I think that she had a problem with me being an equally strong, if not stronger, woman. I don't take shit. She thought she didn't. She just created it—everywhere and long past working for me. This competitive dynamic is unfortunate to watch, and I don't like to be around those sorts of women. I like to help other women succeed, not tear them down.

In any case, as time went on, we had good moments and bad, even moments where I genuinely liked her. But as days turned into months, my unease grew. I had a sense that she was talking about me to others. Even though our team was tight, if you have one weak link it makes the whole group weaker, and when it comes to office culture the person or people who have the bad vibe convert the culture to their level. Eventually, I brought it up to Peter. He had also noticed that she could be rude, dismissive, and flippant around me. As our company was growing, Peter and I moved our desks to another part of the shared office space, the studio in the back, which was actually a converted storage closet. Hey, we needed quiet and space. Our landlord couldn't believe we wanted to actually rent that space, but we did. The joys of working on a shoestring! I was now out of immediate proximity to Lucy, and she could spread her venom more easily without my knowing. Bad idea. That old saying about keeping your friends close and your enemies closer? Right on the money. Not that this girl was strong enough to be an enemy, but moving further away from her was not a smart move. The even-less-smart move was keeping someone around whom I didn't fully trust and didn't like seeing, day in and day out.

Cut to around May 2008. Lucy was still working for Big Think and being more and more disagreeable to me. The other team members were discreetly trying to tell me that there was something amiss with her and that she really had issues with me. They had loyalty to her as a teammate—and outside office hours, even a friend. At that stage, I was still questioning my ability as a manager and leader and so rather than being open and asking for feedback, and, well, advice from others who'd dealt with this sort of thing before, which I should have done, I just tried to plow through and not show weakness. I thought showing others that this was bothering me would make me seem weak. Wrong.

I ignored my feelings because I was insecure in my role. I wasn't sure to what extent being liked was important to me versus commanding respect. You see the dichotomy? Well, it's a false one. It's not one or the other, I've learned. It's being your authentic self no matter the situation. Rising above pettiness is essential to be an effective leader, whether it be about competitiveness, office politics, or anything else. But not being competitive doesn't mean allowing yourself to be treated inappropriately. It doesn't mean ignoring the signs that someone is out to compete with you and create trouble for the whole company in the process. What matters above all else (except kindness) is what you are working to accomplish.

Eventually, the situation came to a head. One of our other employees who had become friends with Lucy outside of work, but was also a good and honorable guy, mentioned something about inappropriate emails being sent on her company account. We would have been within our rights to look at her email right then—as a company, we owned the email accounts—but I didn't. I thought it was an invasion of privacy. If I had looked, she'd have been fired on the spot. Soon after, however, she started posting inappropriate headlines on our website, almost costing us a major sponsor. The time had come to let her go.

Peter was to be the one to fire her, as she seemed volatile and it wasn't clear how she'd handle being fired by me. Well, she didn't handle being fired by Peter so well either. She closed herself in a broom closet, yelling and crying, and started calling staff members asking who had reported her. That evening, I went into her email and saw what she'd been sending to the staff and perhaps even to others outside the organization. It didn't take long before I found that unforgettable three-word descriptor she'd used for me: Liquid Nitrogen C*nt.

Wow.

What I didn't recognize, back then, was that Lucy exhibited all the key attributes of what Big Think expert Bill Eddy calls a "high-conflict person." I need to engrave these reminders on my heart so that I don't make the mistake again of hiring someone who so clearly fits the profile. Eddy explains that HCPs tend to behave in ways that increase conflict rather than reduce or resolve it. The traits he's identified include blaming others (sometimes becoming fixated on one particular individual); all or nothing thinking, which manifests as an inability to compromise; unmanaged emotions, often resulting in outbursts; and extreme behaviors when they perceive themselves to be under threat. HCPs are toxic in a business environment. Period. Don't hire them. And if you do so by mistake, fire them.

NOBODY IS CRITICAL—INCLUDING YOURSELF

When it comes to firing, here's an important lesson I've learned: even if you feel the person is fundamental to the organization, he or she is not. Too many times, I kept people on because I thought they were indispensable and was sometimes even told so by other staff members. This is never the case. Do people often provide or add massive value? Yes. But that doesn't mean the organization can't do without them. It's a fact that if any one person is indispensable once the organization is off the ground, it's not a scalable entity. If you have the notion that the organization would be culturally healthier without that person, or that an individual is making work difficult for others, let that person go. The longer you keep that person, the more poison is spread.

There is often fear that a place will fall apart because of one critical employee, but it just isn't so. Cut them and you will realize nobody is critical. Case in point: Big Think's former chief operating officer.

In 2013, when Big Think was going through a particularly rough patch and Peter was temporarily absent from the office, I hired a COO to come in and help me run Big Think. I desperately needed to be out raising money and selling, and I couldn't do that without help. I turned to Roger, an individual who'd helped us create our first financing deck, way back at the inception of Big Think. He was also Peter's Harvard roommate and a former consultant. He started to work with me as a freelancer, and we worked well together. I genuinely liked him as a person. Over time, I came to rely on him and hired him as our COO.

Much of the time he was at Big Think was great and very productive. He was good with our clients and also with selling and renewals, and he took care of HR matters like contract negotiations. It was a blessing to have him on the team. He and I were working closely together and, though we had different personalities, it worked well. I trusted him and grew to really like him as a friend. The staff let me know how much they appreciated having him on the team, with his fresh perspective and none of the baggage of five years of running a start-up. He put processes in place that had never been there before and provided a much-needed buffer between me and the team.

About two and a half years in, however, I started to have strange feelings about Roger. Things seemed to be slipping through the cracks, emails were not being answered, and there was a fair bit of miscommunication. I felt like important information was being kept from me and things were happening in the company that I wasn't aware of. At first I thought it might be because Roger was in a new, serious relationship and he was distracted. But things didn't improve. I was concerned enough to broach the subject with Peter and one of our advisors. Both of them wanted to support me and so said that whatever I decided would be fine. But I'm loyal to a fault, so I told myself, *This guy came to our company when shit was bad, and I'm going to work it out with him.* That proved to be difficult, however, as our conversations and email exchanges became tense, marked by a growing feeling of unease on my part and a new tone of disrespect and entitlement on his. Increasingly, I wanted him gone, but I'd been told by at least two staff members in the past that if Roger were not part of the team, they would have quit. I was worried that might still be true, and if I fired him, I'd lose them.

The thing is, things change. Life and situations are not static, and I shouldn't have approached this situation as if they were. For some time, I did nothing other than have increasingly detached and uncomfortable conversations with Roger. At about this time, he asked to move out of town and work remotely, as he and his new wife awaited the birth of their son. Instead of taking this as an opportunity to part ways, I said yes, just glad to remove the daily presence of a disgruntled person from the office. For the moment, it seemed it was good for both of us. It wasn't. It really wasn't a tenable move for his senior position. I was unclear what he was doing and felt he was deliberately keeping me out of the loop. I let things slide for a couple more months.

Then, in the summer, individually, three staff members took me aside and told me that they would leave if Roger *wasn't* fired. I couldn't believe it. What a change of story. They all had the same complaint: he'd been hoarding information to ensure that he had knowledge that made him indispensable. He even verbalized this at a staff drinks after I'd left. They each felt that he was not being forthcoming, was delaying work that needed to be done, and was doing the bare minimum. He believed he was indispensable based on the work he'd done, the contacts he'd made, and the knowledge he had of the inner workings of Big Think. He also thought he'd made loyal allies on the team who would protect him. Thing is, most hardworking people don't respect colleagues who don't pull their weight.

I then spoke to each member of the staff and asked what they thought. Turns out, they all wanted him gone. I knew what I had to do. And I was angry. I remember it well. I was sitting in my little midtown apartment, and I called Roger at 9:30 p.m. It was not a normal time to call someone you work with, but too bad. I had already called Peter and told him what I was going to do. Peter immediately alerted our CTO to cut off Roger's accounts so that we had everything before he could go in and start deleting files. I got on the phone with Roger and, for the first and only time in my work history with an employee, I pretty much shouted, "Dude, you are fucking fired." He was obviously shocked and felt ratted out. Sometimes it's good to operate with an element of surprise. He wasn't prepared at all. This was not a pleasant ending to what had once been a stellar working relationship, I'd even say partnership.

This story just shows things can change, even with the best people on your team. You need to operate in the here and now, not basing your choices on how things were or how you wish them to be. Loyalty has its place, but in work, performance and integrity matter way more. I take full responsibility for this. I should have acted immediately rather than let a long time go by out of a sense of loyalty, and frankly, fear of the consequences. I don't do that anymore. Also, while empathy is important, you cannot let it rule you. Sure, be kind when you are letting someone go but do not keep someone around one day longer out of a misguided sense that it's the nicer way. Get that person out immediately.

Another thing to beware of, when it comes to the decision to let someone go, is the "sunk costs fallacy." This is that little voice in your head that says, "We already invested so much in this person, we should try to make the best of it rather than letting him or her go." It's an all-too-common but misguided belief that it's better to hang in there than to cut your losses and move on. Humans fall prey to this way of thinking in many areas of life—from romance to investing to gambling to real estate and definitely in the realm of hiring and firing. Sure, it hurts to see years of training, investment, and knowledge just walk out the door. But it's not worth keeping a toxic individual around.

As soon as I fired Roger, I called every member of our team. When you fire someone, don't forget to pay attention to those who are left behind. It's important not to disturb company culture and to keep the other employees on your side. Let them know that they can trust things will be done in the interest of the company and that they matter. There have been a lot of wonderful people along the way we've let go because they weren't a fit. It's best for them and the company to recognize it soon and (as kindly as possible) let them go.

THE SMELL OF SUCCESS

I couldn't end this chapter without concluding the saga of the smelly feet. Dealing with uncomfortable situations on a day-to-day basis is the norm, whether you are an employee, manager, founder, or CEO. This particular situation arose during a period when, as usual, Big Think had a lot going on and big projects looming. A recent addition to the team was a junior editor, who was part of the booking and interview preparation team.

At the time, teams sat at long communal desks. I was taken aside by two of the women on the team, who sat at that desk or nearby, and told that said new junior editor had very pungent feet, and they couldn't take it. Could I please do something? My first thought was: *Come on! We have deals pending, deliverables due, and this is the issue you need to take me privately into the conference room for?* Well, yes, actually it was. So, I kept my mouth shut and listened. They were looking to me for help and guidance, and that, after all, was and is my role.

They didn't know what to do or how to handle the situation with grace and so they turned to me. It was something I could have laughed off, but I realized something that day: I care about my team and our environment, and that's a fundamental part of my role. The role of a leader, whether in a giant company or a tiny one like ours, is to listen with empathy to anything that is creating a disturbance for the team and to rationally take action to deal with it.

I spoke with the smelly feet offender in a diplomatic way, did not in any way compromise his dignity, and the situation was resolved. I let him know that he was a valued member of our team, and that I appreciated him and his contributions. "I've occasionally been taken aside during my own career," I told him, "for things beyond performance—issues that were more personal. In the moment it felt uncomfortable but I appreciated it, long term." I gave an example—"Victoria, the perfume you wear makes some people nauseous." Not something I had ever considered, and I was chagrined. Then I cut to the chase. "We've got a similar situation with you. Been there, felt that. I know you don't even notice it, but there's an issue with the smell of your feet. It's likely your shoes. No need to be embarrassed—this is trivial stuff. Let's make a change and fix it, okay?"

Now, in many organizations, this is not the kind of thing that has to be done by a CEO, as there would be others to handle it. But the precedent of listening, being caring, and acting in the best interest of the organization is yours to create, across and throughout the organization. And, recognizing and instilling a culture of dignity matters. How you interact with your team and your people actually impacts them as humans. You can increase or decrease someone's dignity in an instant. Think of that, before you speak—whether it's a matter of seeming insignificance or great consequence.

Bottom line, my job as CEO is to help people succeed. At every level of the organization. Whether we be a team of two or a team of thousands. It's the people who matter in an organization. Innovation doesn't happen on its own—it needs to be nurtured, and the people doing the innovating and executing are your people.

Managing people is tough. The most important policy I've learned here is, once again, a big theme of this book: transparency. Set expectations and stick to them. Be direct and clear. Tough is not bad, vacillating and being unclear is the enemy. If you want people to perform, they need to know what you require and how you require it. This does not mean overmanaging—the best work relationships are ones in which employees feel they "own" their job and are constantly growing it and themselves. Helping people grow is the surest way to foster loyalty, engagement, and passion. Am I a perfect boss? No. Am I even a good one? I don't know. What I do know is that almost everyone I've worked with and even fired or let go (and there have been plenty—dozens over the years) respects my honesty and integrity. Very often, years or even months later, they end up calling me for advice. I pull no punches and am clear and direct at every step—and personal. I don't remove my personality from being a boss. I'm human. I'm actually me. And, except in some exceptions when the person has done something unethical or has literally shirked total responsibility, I've tried to nurture my team at Big Think, and even sometimes after they have left. If a person gave time and effort to Big Think, it's the right thing to be helpful to them where possible, even after they have left.

REFLECTIONS

- ◆ Action over words. Know the qualities of the person you want to hire vs. what they say they can do; check for callouses.

- ◆ Beware of Confirmation Bias. We see what we expect to see—and it can set you back.

- ◆ Get rid of high-conflict people. Nobody in the organization is critical—one toxic person will poison the organizational culture.

- ◆ Sunk costs are gone. Don't invest any more in something that isn't working in the hopes that it will.

CHAPTER 5

BOSS NOT B*TCH

Notes on Transitioning from Founder to CEO

One of the key milestones for a fledgling business is that moment when the founder must shift from being the Visionary in Chief to a manager or executive—aka boss. It's a very different role, and many entrepreneurs stumble over this transition, to the detriment of their teams and the business.

What comes to mind when you say the words *founder* or *entrepreneur*? Attributes like creative, innovative, free-thinking, independent, and pioneering are high on many people's lists. Now think about the terms you associate with "boss." *Powerful. Controlling. Successful. Established. In charge.* All of these and more are commonly used to describe bosses.

You can see immediately why it's a leap for the same person to start out as an entrepreneur and then one day wake up to find herself a boss. It can cause quite an identity crisis.

If the boss happens to be a woman, unfortunately there's another word that is often on people's lips—also beginning with B. I'll admit, over the years I've made a lot of mistakes being the "boss" and yes, sometimes I have come off as being a bitch. I truly don't like that word, but it is often how people describe female leaders—as the shrewish, controlling harpy. Largely that isn't true; it's a public perception, a misnomer, but once in a while it can be true. I think that when women are insecure about their own leadership capacities or are convinced that to lead, they need to act like men, they inadvertently become their own worst selves. I've certainly fallen into that trap.

Deservedly or not, people use that term as shorthand for some of the least attractive female attributes. So, I'd like to share what I've learned (sometimes the hard way) about how to avoid adding to that perception of women in power, and instead use some of the most positive female attributes to help you become a better boss, whether you're male or female.

Women are known as nurturers. And, in building and growing a business, this is a positive. In my humble opinion, leadership is not about command and control: that's for the army. When I first became a "boss," I mistakenly adopted the command-and-control type of leadership. It didn't feel right, but I thought it was what I was supposed to do. I truly felt that for my people to respect me, I had to show unwavering strength and be the commander in chief, especially as a woman. I thought men had more leeway to be nice and caring, but that if I nurtured people, they would lose respect for me. Or I would never gain it in the first place.

This turned out to be totally wrong. A business is not an army, and the concept of "controlling" them will not get the best out of people. Along the way, I have learned that the opposite is true. I think I've come to use *nurturing* as my most useful asset or quality as a leader. For me, I find it gets the best out of my team and also allows me to be myself and not some stereotypical female CEO who just seems like a woman pretending to be a man. I also avoid becoming the stereotypical worst type of male leader—controlling, unempathetic, bullying. Most male bosses are not that, but it's a common misconception that that's how a successful CEO behaves. Of course, every boss is different. For some, the command and control type of system may, at least temporarily, yield results. I'm just not sure it will fare well for the organization in the long run.

Being nurturing does not mean being a softy. For me, it just means leading authentically, and by nature I am a nurturer. One way that is expressed is in nurturing the reasons my team work for the company. They didn't come to work for us just to get ordered around and sent home with a paycheck. Something about the company, its values, its ethos, and its mission spoke to them. Understand what those reasons are and communicate them. Regularly and openly. Nurture that alignment of individual and organizational missions, and you won't need to command or control anyone.

COMMUNICATION IS EVERYTHING

One of the most critical areas for an organization is internal communication—does the left hand know what the right hand is doing? Creating silos will kill you. That builds a culture where people are focusing on what I do, as opposed to what *we* do. Acting in one's own self-interest rather than the organization's interest takes you into a less-than-desirable reward/punishment system. The individual is rewarded for performance above what's actually achieved for the organization. Think about it like this: there are finite resources to make the company run effectively, and they must be shared. Sometimes one part of the organization needs more of the resources for a particular reason but no one portion can be fully cut off—it's like cutting off the blood supply that every portion of the body needs. If individuals are being rewarded solely on their own performance, they are motivated to take or use as much of the resources as they can, possibly to the detriment of the entire organism.

It's important to note that for all of us, the reward/punishment system in which we are enmeshed professionally largely controls behavior. People are constantly trying to ascertain what is required of them and how they will be rewarded, and then working to achieve that reward. The critical thing to understand is that often they are operating from the wrong system—not out of malice but simply because they do not know what is wanted of them or the overarching goal of the organization.

How is it possible that people don't know what their role is and, perhaps even more important, the objective of the company? As Robert S. Kaplan and David P. Norton write in *Harvard Business Review*, "Our research reveals that, on average, 95 percent of a company's employees are unaware of, or do not understand, its strategy."[1] How can people know what to do to help the company succeed if they don't even know the company goals? And how can this situation happen? There are a whole bunch of ways this disconnect can happen.

In the early years of Big Think, we didn't have a mission statement. We knew what we were about—at least, we thought we did—but we didn't often express that to the team. And the team was changing all the time. Over the last twelve years, we've likely had more than a hundred people full-time at Big Think and hundreds of freelancers. Every single one of these people needed to be inspired by what we were trying to achieve for them to deliver their best performance. While I thought Peter and I could describe Big Think in a clear way, I realized when I listened to team members describe us that they were all saying something different. That's not how you drive mission. Everybody needs to be able to recite the mission statement in their sleep. To achieve this, the mission needs to be verbalized often in the organization and written down. Sure, it can develop and evolve, but at each and every moment, it must be clear.

Even with the mission crystal clear, it's still too easy to miscommunicate. Case in point: our mission at Big Think is to help people get smarter, faster. We are about knowledge, not opinion. I thought I had clearly communicated this, but a few years ago it came to my attention that one of our writers was continually writing about politics. The content was getting a lot of traffic, but it was not representative of our mission. I was alerted to this after several articles had gone on the site without my noticing. This particular situation was problematic because at the time, we had a sponsor who had explicitly told us that one of the main reasons they sponsored Big Think was because of our brand's association with knowledge and not opinion.

I called our managing editor, Orion, who was in charge of the freelance writers, and got pretty upset with him. In an (unnecessarily) angry tone, I said: "Orion, come on! You know our mission is to help people get smarter, faster. It is *not* about opinion. Why did you allow this article to be published?! It's not okay! Our sponsor has noticed and is not happy and is threatening to remove the sponsorship. This is bad!"

Quite calmly, he responded: "Victoria, you said at the last staff meeting that traffic to the site was paramount, and we each needed to do whatever it took to increase it. I spoke with all of our writers and told them this, so they did research on what topics drive the most traffic—and politics and opinion and vitriol are pretty high up there. I'm sorry that you are upset and that the sponsor is upset, but you said '*anything*,' and I took you at your word."

My bad. He heard the goal was traffic at all costs. Plus, every writer was paid by the article and by a traffic bonus, so of course they would do whatever they could to maximize that. Since I, apparently, had told them they could, of course they did. We rectified the situation pretty quickly, but it's a cautionary example of what can happen when a leader's communication of the reward/punishment system isn't clear, and how the business can suffer as a result.

Deviations from the mission are often made a quarter of a degree at a time, so you never see the reality of the change in direction until you've totally departed from your objective. This can be prevented through culture and an effective and clear reward/punishment system. Punishment sounds bad, I get it. But it essentially just means establishing the consequences of not following our mission, which is clearly stated and apparent to all.

For many, one of the key questions about being a boss is this: how to be an authority figure to those who don't necessarily want to be around authority? But it's not actually about authority at all, it's about inspiration. To get the best from yourself and others, inspiration and mission are key.

So, how do you inspire your employees? First and foremost, by ensuring that you are inspired yourself. If you aren't excited and pumped up for the work ahead, those around you won't be either. It's easy for minutiae to creep in and drag you down. Giving yourself and those around you permission to dream will catalyze innovation and ultimately increase performance. Staying inspired can mean something different for everybody. For me, I need a regular change of scenery and sometimes a total change of pace. I work best under intense pressure, which I'm very used to, but sometimes I must change this to regenerate. When I started Big Think, the inspiration gave me confidence. I didn't ask permission or direction; I just went out and did it. Passing on this inspiration to others and the freedom to execute it (within reason) is something that will help you and your people achieve their goals and find joy and satisfaction in the process.

LOCATION, LOCATION, LOCATION

When it comes to culture and communication, location matters. Big Think moved into a new office space in 2009. In our old space on 5th Avenue there really hadn't been space for the whole staff to sit together. We were renting nooks and crannies around a shared office. Peter and I, and our then editorial chairman, shared one small room, the production team was in the studio, and the editors and tech people sat together. It worked out all right, but it did create a separation between the units, which meant that communication between them was not optimal and sometimes there was drastic miscommunication. Additionally, I was separated from the team, so I wasn't getting all the information I needed. People felt nervous to come and talk with me and Peter, as if they were coming to the principal's office. It was not my intention, but I also became more comfortable being sequestered. So, when we moved to our new office on 17th Street, out of habit, Peter and I separated ourselves into the conference room, which had glass doors that could be closed. The rest of the team sat in the open office space together.

Sometime after this arrangement was made, I realized that we were making people uncomfortable. They were less likely to come and talk with us because it seemed more formal. Additionally, they felt awkward about asking to use the conference room for meetings. If I'm honest with myself, I was a little annoyed when I was asked to move, and I'm sure people picked up on that. All in all, it was a bad decision. How can I lead, if I'm not in the midst? I've been to offices where the CEO literally has his or her own floor and manages from on high Even if the CEO does a regular walk around, it feels like a checkup and people get scared. That's not the kind of culture I want to create in my company.

I've found that people, whether employees or partners, clients or our experts, respect the CEO or founder when they get down in the dirt. When I'm at the office and have a guest coming, I always greet people by the elevator. I manage my own schedule and email so I can be personal and in control to the greatest extent possible and show people I care about them as humans beyond business. That's not to say every CEO should work without an assistant—for some people, a good assistant actually helps them to stay on top of their communications and ensure that people feel heard. My point is simply that people are always looking to the boss for signals. And how you relate to your people is critical.

One of my professors at HBS, Tom DeLong, taught me a simple but profound lesson that I've never forgotten. "Ambiguity is always perceived negatively," he said. He gave an example about how one day he was hurrying to his next class when a student came up to him and wanted to talk with him about something casually. DeLong sort of acknowledged the student but kept moving and not really engaging. He reflected on it later and realized that the student may have interpreted his actions really badly and spiraled into negative thoughts. *Holy shit, does Professor DeLong not like me? Am I doing badly in his class? Am I going to fail?* Meanwhile, all the professor was doing was rushing to his next class. That has always stuck with me—*ambiguity is always interpreted negatively.* I try to remember this in my interactions, but I don't always succeed. As a boss, I do think it's important to reflect on those ambiguous interactions and try to rectify them if you can and make clear what was happening. And ask for suggestions for how you might have handled it better. Make it easy for people to come to you, make yourself available in spirit.

Big Thinkers Say . . .

In his Big Think interview, the actor Alan Alda emphasizes the art of listening as the key to good communication. "I think communication is a partnership," he says. "You have to think about your partner and help your partner. It's not me pouring stuff into your empty brain. First of all, you've got plenty of stuff in there already that I ought to want to know about."[2]

The better you relate, the better you will communicate, but if you are separate you cannot actually relate. That doesn't always mean you have to physically be in the same location, but the culture must be one of openness and unity. In many instances, I haven't listened to what a colleague or employee is saying—concerned that I needed to stay within the zone of always "being in charge." That's not okay. As the leader, you need to create a forum for your team to contribute and express issues. If you isolate yourself, you will not actually know what's going on. And, frankly, the concept of "being in charge," I've come to realize, is a stupid concept. If this is the way you deal with your team—for example, speak when I want you to speak, as opposed to when the person wants or needs to—you will miss out on so much that you need to hear. Whether they have an issue, an idea, or something personal to talk about, or just a need for some of your time to show they matter, give it. And to do so, you must make yourself available—in whatever form that takes for you and the organization. You cannot be walled off and unapproachable.

STRATEGY IS SITUATION SPECIFIC

While a company's vision and mission remain essentially unchanging, the strategies by which it pursues that mission must constantly be updated. Just because something works in one setting doesn't mean it will work in a different one. As a leader, you always need to figure out the context. For instance, you may have had the greatest cavalry and seemed set for victory, but what if the other side suddenly has tanks? That's a whole new battlefield. The context has totally changed, and so must your and your team's approach. Repeating something that worked in the past will often lead to failure.

Throughout Big Think's history, it's been my job to notice the context and change. For instance, early on, our business model was entirely based on sponsorship and advertising. It worked for us for a couple years, but then came the economic crisis that started in 2008. Advertising budgets dried up and continuing to pitch the same concept to the same entities (advertising agencies and corporations) would have spelled our financial ruin. Indeed, we came very close. So, we created products that we thought would be well received in the corporate and educational space—a licensing product for e-learning. That saved our hide in the short term when we could sell no sponsorships and our traffic was not significant enough for major advertising dollars. Recently, we've noticed that the context has changed again, and advertising and sponsorships are once again more viable and can legitimately form a meaningful portion of our revenue. Do we pitch the same sorts of ideas as we did early on? Not exactly. We've evolved, as we've seen what will sell and we continue to try to be ahead of the curve.

Being the boss and making those types of calls can be lonely sometimes. It's both empowering and daunting to have everybody looking to you to make decisions and lay out the roadmap. There's often a misguided sense that the boss controls outcomes, which contributes to this. That's rarely the case. Yes, leaders can make decisions, but they can't control if business is good or bad, beyond following the mission and doing the best they can. Being accountable personally for things like payroll, customer satisfaction, employee satisfaction, investor return, and so many other things is really stressful. There have been countless times when I felt alone in dealing with these matters. I am the person looking at our bank account every day and forecasting worst-case scenarios. And let me tell you, it's fucking scary. I'm the person required to make the tough decisions and then execute them. Sometimes I've done well, sometimes badly. And guess what? Either way it ends up, you're the fall guy. Good or bad.

I've had to lay off many people—not because they failed or fell short, but just because we had to cut costs if we were to survive. I know it's hard being on the receiving end of one of those meetings. What I hadn't appreciated until being in the position myself is that it's also really hard on the person delivering the bad news. And, nobody wants to do it. I dread having those meetings when it needs to be done. I don't like letting people down, especially those who have contributed to what we do. And yet, at times it's essential. It's for the good of the business. I have to remind myself, again and again, I have a fiduciary responsibility. While I want to make people happy, my number-one responsibility is to create an environment where the business is most likely to succeed. I'm a human with a beating heart, too, and I believe in being kind and empathetic, so these times are tough. Unfortunately, I've been through them a lot. In a start-up situation with not a lot of funding, it's inevitable—unless you are way off the bell curve. And, this leads me to my next point. Good or bad, finding the solution to a challenge or an opportunity is always your job. The buck stops with you. Always and repeatedly.

It has become clear to me, over time, that effective solutions are a product of my positive energy. Most often, the solution will not be something I've thought of alone, but something inspired by what I've heard from a team member or an advisor, or something totally out of the blue. In order to receive that inspiration, you need to be rested and clear. Detaching from things, like Bill Gates does, is a good idea. He goes away for a week every year just to read, be alone, and expose himself to new ideas. Though I'm no Bill Gates (I'd like to be!), I also work to detach myself from the day-to-day to get new perspective. I need to grow and be better to help those around me do the same. To be always learning and growing is essential as a boss, and it's imperative to show that you require it from your team. Things that stagnate, die.

HELP PEOPLE GROW, UP THEIR GAME, AND TRANSFORM

At Big Think, I've encouraged people to better themselves, take classes, and move into roles that they were not necessarily hired for. About four years ago, we hired a junior employee whose role was primarily in client success—taking care of the current client roster we had. She excelled in this role for about a year and a half and clients loved her, but she wanted to become an expert in marketing. She had no experience but told me how important it was to her.

I said: "Okay, what can we do to make this work? You're in this one role now, you've become great at it, and we don't have anyone to take your place—plus we don't have the resources to hire and train someone to replace you now. But I hear what you want, and I want you to grow. What do you propose?"

She suggested taking some classes on marketing and beginning to work on some projects in that area while maintaining her client success role and looking to find someone who could eventually take over. I agreed.

She upped her game. She learned about marketing, started to practice, continued in her client success role, and grew massively. She had a whole new skill set that was increasing daily. It was remarkable, but not surprising. It's the way humans are. As a boss, if you let people step out of their comfort zone they grow exponentially for themselves and for the organization. Doing the same thing over and over will not inspire people. Inspiration is key. Allow people to have fun, encourage enjoyment, and require growth.

BIG BOSSES DO CRY

"If you don't show up, it could be the end for our company."

I knew the emotion of the moment came through in my voice, but I didn't care. This was not a moment to try to hold up an image of stereotypical CEO toughness. All I could do was appeal to the woman on the other end of the phone not to let us down, because if she did, we'd let our sponsor down, they wouldn't pay us, and we'd have to lay off all our staff and shut down our thought-leadership platform. I laid it on thick, because it was true. Everything rested on the success of this event, and this woman—a key speaker—was threatening to bail.

The year was 2010, and after several months of hard work, Big Think had secured a major sponsorship from Shell for its Eco Warrior event. It involved us running two live events in Houston, one of which was a panel discussion featuring environmental experts, including notable VC Vinod Khosla, the global CEO of Shell, and others.

The problem with these kinds of events is that you're depending on people to show up. And unless you have a big budget to make it worth their time, shit can go south, and there is literally no guarantee your panelists will be there on the day. However, we'd done our homework and felt pretty good about the lineup we'd prepared. Then, about ten days before the event, Shell dropped a bombshell. They didn't have an audience and had thought that this was part of our offering. Uh, no. Not something we were expecting at all, and quite frankly not something we had experience doing. However, this was a very important account, and we desperately needed the money. So, we became event planners, with me as the event-planner-in-chief, making it clear to our team that this was something we *would* achieve. We were going up, over, under, or around the mountain, but we sure as heck were conquering it. And we did. It involved some creativity to get two hundred people to attend a midweek lunch in Houston, a city in which we had no connections. But because failure was not an option, we pulled it off.

The lunch event was being livestreamed by the *Houston Chronicle*. We thought we had it all under control, when a key woman on the panel (the only woman in fact), who was flying in from D.C., called me on the morning of the event, leaving a voicemail to tell me she had decided not to come. Thank goodness I listened to it, as I didn't recognize the number. In that moment, I could have panicked, but instead I sprang into action. I did feel the panic but I pushed it aside. I called her and literally begged her to come. I was brutally honest about what was on the line. My team saw me in a way they hadn't before—appealing to someone's humanity. I knew she still did not want to come and there was nothing in it for her (except the networking opportunity), but she listened to me and, because I was authentic, she got on that plane. Leadership manifests itself at different times in different ways. And as a leader you need to figure out what role you need to play in each situation. Sometimes, being boss just means being a vulnerable human being.

REFLECTIONS

◆ Earn respect, don't command it.

◆ The office isn't the military—people need to want to be there and to perform.

◆ Get in the mix. Separating yourself from your team will lead to miscommunication. Make yourself available.

◆ Be You. It's most effective (and pleasurable) to lead authentically.

CHAPTER 6

WORK IT

·····················

The Advantages
of Being the Only
Woman in the Room

Let's get this straight: being an entrepreneur isn't easy. For anybody. As a female founder and CEO, I'll confess I get tired of being asked the "woman" questions—but let's get them out of the way.

How do you handle the work-life balance? Answer: I don't! (Want more detail? I give the lowdown on my love life in Chapter 7).

Do you worry that as a strong female CEO you'll intimidate men? Answer: uh, no, but I'm sure it happens. It's just not something for me to worry about. I need to invest most of my energy in my performance as a leader.

Have you ever been harassed or discriminated against? Answer: probably. But if so, it's been minor and I've been willfully oblivious and not focused on it. Let's be clear: sexual harassment in the workplace is obviously a big deal. It damages women and often the companies they work for, since they may be losing excellent talent due to a culture with an unacceptable tolerance for harassment. I don't take that lightly. But in the minor incidents I've experienced, mostly involving men over sixty-five, it wouldn't have served me to call attention to them. I needed to focus on opportunity, not on challenge (or in these cases, small indiscretions), in order to do what I've done. I've been responsible for the majority of fundraising and investor relations at Big Think, and most of our investors and potential investors are male. And, on the whole, my many encounters with powerful men, in business and beyond, have been free of bad behavior. Men, by and large, are good people. They are getting a lot of crap these days en masse because of the behavior of a select few. The majority of the investors in my company have become not only advisors but personal mentors as well. As for the few incidents where older men have behaved in small but harmless (to me) sexist ways that are outside of today's norms, I chalk it up to them being used to a different time and culture and not having grasped what is and isn't appropriate. Maybe that's an overly generous interpretation, but it's worked for me.

If older men I'm working with call me "honey" or "dear," I let it slide. Culture changes, and not everybody catches up, but they don't necessarily mean harm or even disrespect. A lot of the people who have invested in me and coached me come from a different era. The business landscape has dramatically changed since they began their careers. Some of them may have gone through significant parts of their professional lives largely without the presence of women colleagues, other than secretaries, and were groomed by men before them who were even more out of tune with the concept of female professionals. Behavior that we may rightly deem inappropriate today may have been perfectly normal during most of their careers. Should they update? Yes, ideally. But change is hard for any of us, especially when old habits have had decades of practice. Many men have transitioned well into a world where women no longer merely play supporting roles. But others have found it more of a challenge and may not necessarily understand that some of their behavior and language is "off."

I have empathy for that. And I approach situations where I know (or at least sense) the man has good intentions and wants to be helpful with an open mind. Rather than rushing to judgment, I recognize good intent and don't let the small stuff bother me. Yes, some men relate differently to me than they would, say, to my business partner. They may use terms of endearment that aren't perceived as respectful today. There is also sometimes a tendency to treat me as if I needed protection. That's fine. But I understand that sometimes it's a generational thing, not a misogynistic thing. I don't shame them for it. And I don't let it derail a positive, professional relationship.

Honestly, am I going to give up a million dollars and the chance to save my company because someone has called me "honey"? Who is actually the loser in that scenario? I'm not giving men a free pass. I know the behavior isn't right, but I have an understanding for changing times. If a man in his forties were to behave in a similar way, I'd take it totally differently and address it head-on. And, by the way, men are not the only ones who use inappropriate language about women, professionally. There are plenty of women, under fifty, who call other women "sweetie," and they aren't serving you a cup of coffee in a diner.

Of course, serious harassment or abuse by anyone, at any age, is another matter, and I'm thankful to say I've never had to deal with that. I know many women aren't so lucky and sometimes find themselves in near-impossible positions when power is in play. Personally, I never found myself in a position where anything too serious could happen. There have been times where I could have compromised my own principles because we needed the money or the sale or whatever, but in the end, my self-worth and integrity have always mattered more.

This is a line I've walked my entire career. And it's been my experience that, even in the midst of inappropriate behavior, things can be shut down in a nonaggressive, effective way that makes my boundaries clear but doesn't shut people out.

Don't get me wrong—some of these guys might have deserved a more direct response. But I'm always trying to do what's best for the business, without compromising in ways that matter. There have been countless times when I've had to suck it up when men made misogynistic or belittling remarks, and not get pissy about it. Pissy won't get you money. Pissy is also an ineffective way to catalyze change. You need to get people to want to help you, not get people to not want to be around you.

If you get pissy, it will reinforce the bad behavior as well as the misconceptions about women. To get things to change, you need to encourage new behavior and help people understand why your differences are good. Do I like having to do this? Not really. But I care more about being effective. Countless times over the years, I've gone into meetings with Peter and had the people in the room (yes, even the women) look to him as the decision-maker. Getting angry about it doesn't help. Calm confidence is the answer. And humor, when appropriate. People like to laugh and by and large are good-natured.

Sometimes, laughing it off makes you more interesting to be around, and if you can do it effectively, you can emerge stronger personally, with a good relationship, and get what you want. Breaking these barriers is doable and it's possible to do it in a positive way. In today's hypersensitive culture, I see too many women reacting with outrage when humor or even compassion might have served them better and put them in a more authentically powerful position. Again, abuse or harassment is never a laughing matter, but it's not always a crime to be a little out of step with the times.

It's taken me many years and more than a few missteps to learn how to handle uncomfortable encounters with humor or even grace. In my early days at Big Think, sometimes my brash and pushy attitude got me into situations that required a hasty exit. Case in point? The time I decided to pitch to a Canadian business tycoon who had a bit of a reputation for being, well—let's just say it was years before the #MeToo movement, and I was quite a bit younger. We needed money, so I found his email and contacted him and told him I was coming to Toronto and had an investment pitch for him. I was staying at my parents' house and my father insisted on driving me to the meeting. The tycoon lived in a fancy residential neighborhood, in a big Asian-themed house. I got out of the car and told my dad I'd see him later. Little did I know, he waited in the car because he knew this guy's reputation too. If I was in there for more than forty-five minutes, he intended to knock on the door.

I rang the bell, and the potential investor answered the door in a robe. Yes, a robe. "Hello, come in," he said, as if this was nothing unusual. He brought me into the kitchen and asked if I would like a glass of vodka. It was 11:00 a.m. I declined but he kept insisting as he poured himself a shot and one for me too. He then said he'd be right down after he took a shower and we could talk business. I waited in the kitchen, and poured the shot down the drain. About fifteen minutes later he came down. This guy was about sixty, with slicked-back hair, now dressed in what I suppose he thought was hip attire.

He filled the glasses again and said, "Come on, let's go outside." He told me his wife was away and that we had ample time to talk. We walked out to his koi pond. Yes, a koi pond, in the middle of Toronto. He offered me a joint. I don't smoke pot, and I certainly wasn't going to do so with him. He talked about himself for some time and name-dropped, and I was beginning to feel that this was a pointless meeting, all about his ego. Perhaps he just hoped I'd be amenable to something more than just business. He wanted me to stay for lunch and continue talking, but I declined and left. My dad was still waiting outside.

The point of all this is that, yes, I got the meeting and interest from a very wealthy individual, but it was a dangerous road to go down. Not getting what I was pushing for turned out to be a gift. Having that guy associated with Big Think would not have served our brand well, and I would likely have been placed in compromising positions over and over. At least I stopped at that point and didn't press for another meeting. I cut bait. Sometimes in moments of need, I've been pushy and brash at the wrong time, with the wrong people. I knew in my gut this was a person I didn't want to be associated with, and I pushed anyway. I've since learned, even in times of sincere business need, to not ever do anything that I would be ashamed of. I often ask myself, at moments like that, "If things were going well with the business, would you do this?" If the answer is no, walk away.

Anyway, enough about misbehaving men. As I said, I get tired of answering the "woman" questions, and I wish people asked me the questions they ask any male CEO as frequently—What are the secrets to your success? How did you persevere through the tough times? What do you want to achieve next? I'd be happier talking about the challenges all entrepreneurs face, such as catalyzing innovation, raising capital, growth, competition, and leadership. And yet, we can't seem to escape the gender issues. Perhaps that isn't surprising, given that in 2018, women led only twenty-four of the Fortune 500 companies (that's 4.8 percent, down from a high of 6.4 percent in 2017), female founders received only 2.2 percent of US venture capital ($2.3 billion out of a total $96.7 billion), and women still earned 80 cents for every dollar their male counterparts earn (a collective loss of more than $500 billion). And that's before we even get started on the ever-elusive work-life balance. So, I guess we do still need to talk about gender. But since everyone's talking about the negatives, I'd like to focus on the other side of the picture. What are the benefits of being a woman in business, and how can you, I, and even our male colleagues benefit?

THE NEW POWER SUIT

Let's be honest: the rules are different for men and women. If you're a woman, looks matter, as do charm, presentation, and grace. No one really cares what a guy looks like or even acts like when he makes a pitch—they just want to know if he can deliver on the business plan. But women are scrutinized for their physical appearance and their tone. (Why do you think Elizabeth Holmes adopted that weird-as-fuck low voice?) Would I like this reality to be different? Sure. But it's not. And I'd rather win at the business game than claim a foul because I have to dress up in more than a hoodie and flip-flops for a pitch meeting.

It's a mistake to think we can—or should—banish sexual dynamics and differences from the workplace completely. That may end up serving neither women nor men. I know this concept will make some people uncomfortable, but the innate qualities of men and women are different. To what degree are those differences a result of our biology? And to what degree are they enculturated? That's a topic for another kind of book. My point is simply this: let's celebrate them and learn how to harness them effectively.

One of the key differences—and I'm aware that I'm making a generalization, but it's true enough to be worth making—is that women have more freedom and opportunity to leverage their physical appearance. That's right: freedom and opportunity. I know we can tell the story another way—women are unfairly judged on their looks, women are objectified, and so on. That's true too. But many women, myself included, love fashion and femininity. It's fun, creative, and empowering to dress in something that makes you feel good. And I would argue that in this day and age, women are given more freedom to do so at work than men, and that's a good thing. So, take advantage! Find your style and work it.

Every woman has a different definition of comfort. While some women love themselves some Dr. Scholl's paired with a nice set of shoulder pads, I personally prefer to follow the trends. The key words, for me, are *stylish* and *youthful*. I don't mean I'm trying to be young, but I've gotta have an open spirit, a joie de vivre, to live a little on the edge. For many, being all buttoned up is the stereotype of a professional businesswoman. I say it's kind of boring, but for some women, that's what makes them comfortable, and that's okay. You do you. I dress up, and, as Big Think expert Amy Cuddy would suggest, adopt power positions. What that means is that I dress to feel attractive, comfortable, confident, and authentic. I don't own any pantsuits and would never wear one, even to a meeting with bankers, because that's just not me. If that's your personal style, then by all means, rock it. But don't just wear what you think you should in order to fit in.

The last thing I want when going into meetings or other important business events is to not feel like myself. I've learned this the hard way. Case in point? It wasn't really the outfit, it was the face. A black eye, a bruised and road-burned cheekbone, and a fat lip. Accompanying all this was a sling, a limp, and a pair of heels, clearly making the limp worse. I'd tried to at least achieve a modicum of professional style after an unfortunate tumble during a run—God bless the New York City streets. I'd tripped on a manhole and slammed into the middle of an intersection, face and shoulder first. I'm lucky I didn't break my jawbone. Big Think was scheduled to host an event the next morning with the renowned psychotherapist and relationship expert Esther Perel at the hip communal working space NeueHouse, in Manhattan's Flatiron District. Peter would be interviewing her about some of her recent work on relationships between business partners, ours being the one to talk about that day. I felt I had to show up.

When I arrived, I was already in pain, made more uncomfortable by my "professional" clothing. I had thought that the outfit was somehow masking the disaster of my physical reality. No. I'd have been better with just looser clothing and flat shoes. I could have been presentable without compounding the effects of my injuries. By dressing in a way that enhanced my discomfort, I made my situation all the more noticeable.

If you look good and are comfortable in what you are wearing, you feel good. Know your audience. There's nothing wrong with dressing for them. In fact, it's actually *suitable*. No shame. It's representing yourself. Why lose qualities that make you special and different and can contribute to your success and the success of others? Dress in the suit that makes you feel your best self. Often that isn't your sexiest self; it's your attractive, engaging, powerful self.

TONE IT UP

Here's another male-female disparity that I think you can use to your advantage: tone. I recognize that men speak differently to women, and when there's a female presence in a meeting, it's probably going to have a slightly different tone than when it's all men. Good! Use it. This is an opportunity to be authentic. For me, that means I like to banter and be light. I like wordplay and humor, and I don't take that part of myself out of meetings. It's often why, even if we don't get the deal or whatever it is we're working toward, I forge lasting relationships with people in business. They actually want to be around me. It's not just win or lose—the process is what matters. Truly. And enjoying the process—for me, anyway—means showing up as me, not as some constructed version of myself.

Here's an example: I'd been invited to one of our investors' annual summer parties. The host is the former CEO of a major media/technology company and a lovely man. I'd been going to this party for several years, and I knew it would be filled with leading businesspeople, politicians, former New York chiefs of police, media tycoons, and people who run (or used to run) major companies and initiatives. I decided that day to skip going home and changing into a dress—which is what the majority of women at the party would be wearing—and instead to wear something a little more comfortable. I arrived in a pair of fitted jeans, ripped at the knee (as is the style these days—check out the supermodels) as well as a crisp white shirt and, you got it, some cool boots. I looked stylish and sophisticated yet still felt comfortable. And I stood out.

I was not trying to impress anybody with what I was wearing, I just showed up in what I knew to be attractive for me. I walked through the crowded party and met my business partner and several others standing in a little circle. Toward the end of the terrace was a bar, so I headed over to get a glass of rose. En route, I passed an older man I recognized—the deputy chairman and managing director of a notable international bank. I'd met him several times through the host of the event and he'd been helpful and kind to me, so I stopped to say hello to him and his wife.

He looked me up and down. "Victoria, if you are so hard up that you can't afford to buy a pair of jeans without rips, I will buy you a pair."

In this moment, I had a choice. I could have been insulted, embarrassed, or made to feel like I was not part of the "scene." Or, I could take it as an opportunity to present myself authentically. I did the latter. I laughed and said, "Thanks, I'd like that. I'll send you a link to the ones I want via email."

He was clearly taken aback, and his wife seemed surprised. I could tell she thought I was a bit of an upstart. But he said, "You do that!"

As I was about to continue to the bar, a tall, well-dressed man who had been standing nearby turned to speak with me. "That was funny," he said. "I was impressed by how you handled it." He introduced himself and asked about what I did. I told him the story of Big Think, and he was interested and took my number. We chatted the following week, and he's since become another trusted advisor who has introduced me personally, and the company, to dozens of top companies and notable people. That would never have happened if I'd just let myself feel embarrassed or put down.

Being charming, authentic, and humorous in situations that may not feel comfortable has often proven to create opportunities for me. I never did get the jeans though, even though I sent a link to the $900 pair I wanted—I thought I'd make a little statement with that. The lesson here is to be brash when the situation calls. If people smack you down, smack back. Hopefully you won't need to, because you will command power and respect, as I have done over the course of my career with many influential men who are not known for being easy to deal with. If you can be truly comfortable with who you are and be bold when the time is right, then you can harness a confidence and power that can truly work to your advantage.

At the same party a couple years earlier, I spotted Vikram Pandit, the former CEO of Citi. I told my COO I had to go and talk with him. My COO was nervous and didn't want to do a cold self-introduction. I had no such reservations. I walked up to him while he was in the midst of conversation with a few others. I waited patiently and smiled and when there was a pause, introduced myself and gave him the thirty-second elevator pitch—and was charming about it. Here's another benefit to being a woman—most men aren't used to women doing this type of introduction, and while they might be annoyed when other men do it, they are more likely to listen to a woman. From that cold intro, Vikram introduced us to his chief of staff and they invested in Big Think.

AIN'T TOO PROUD TO LEARN

Confidence is power, and I use every asset at my disposal to maximize my own confidence in business situations. However, there have inevitably been times when I've felt less than confident, or I was just having a bad day, and that's when mentors can provided needed support and encouragement. Larry Summers is a brilliant man, but not exactly known for being easygoing. I have always felt I can be myself around him: open, vulnerable, and turned up to the max. He respects that and is totally blunt with me, personally and professionally. I see that as a gift.

In 2015, I'd invited a bunch of our investors, advisors, and some other notable folks to join Peter, myself, and other team members for a brainstorming session about the future of Big Think, over lunch at Milos in New York. The impressive guest list included Larry Summers, David Stern, chairman emertis of the NBA, John Seely Brown, Carla Newman, Tom Scott, former Bloomberg CEO Lex Fenwick, notable couples therapist and Big Think regular Esther Perel, and former ABC president David Westin. I'd arranged the whole thing. I'd forged strong relationships with all the men and the two other women at the table. I'd managed to get them to root for me, not just for their financial success. They wanted me to succeed. Why? I can't say for sure, but I think it was because of my authenticity.

At that time, I'd been having a pretty rough couple weeks, having not closed some sales I was hoping for, and watching our funds dwindle in the bank. But guess what? This was an important lunch and I intended to make it valuable for all attendees and especially for Big Think and, ultimately, its investors. In the CEO role, I'm used to being the person all eyes are on. But seated in a private dining room with these powerhouses, desperately worried about our financial situation, I was not feeling all that confident. I'd prepared something to say to greet people, but I was dreading it.

Before we got started, I was chatting with Tom Scott and Lex Fenwick casually. I said that I was really nervous and didn't like giving talks. Both of these men, so used to public speaking, were encouraging. Not in a babying or condescending way, but in a genuine, supportive manner. "Victoria what you have built is incredible, own it, stand up and welcome the people who support you and start the dialogue of this lunch."

Well, I did so—incredibly badly. I am not usually one to suffer from nerves (or at least, I hadn't been prior to this).

I sure did that day. I stood up and literally said five words of the speech I had prepared to catalyze conversation and start a meaningful engagement. I turned bright red and sat down abruptly. I could sense people looking at me with a mix of concern and confusion: "What the fuck is this all about?" But these were all nice people and so they plowed ahead and engaged in the discussion. Our COO took over where I left off, thank God, and the lunch began but not without, on my part, a deep sense of shame and embarrassment.

As testament to my increasingly mentor-like relationship with Larry, he said "In honor of Victoria, content is, once again, Queen. How do we capitalize on this and help her and Big Think?" Brilliant—a very kind way to once again include me, as I could tell that he knew something was off. I had thought I'd have to stand up and opine, and he just catalyzed meaningful dialogue for me. He took over. It was in no way aggressive; it was a gift and for me a learning experience. That's what those who truly help people grow are able to do. They lead by example. They do the work and show you how it's done.

Cut to several weeks later. I was in Palo Alto for business meetings when I received an email from one of Larry's assistants asking to set up a call with him. *Uh oh.* What does Larry want to talk about? Of course. The lunch. I knew well enough that my participation would be called into question as well as the whole darn thing itself. Larry pulled no punches. He told me that I'd misled people about what the lunch was about—which was true, though not out of any ill intent on my part. I'd allowed it to morph into something that it was not originally supposed to be. It was supposed to be a brainstorming session to generate ideas and perhaps even clear plans of how Big Think could scale, and what each of the attendees could do to help. Instead, it became much more of a promotional lunch for Big Think, with the hopes of raising more money. Perhaps this ambiguity had something to do with my dramatic lack of confidence and inability to simply be authentic in the situation. Transparency is strength.

However, instead of calling me out for wasting his time, which would have been fair enough, Larry wanted to give me some schooling, which I needed. He told me I'd essentially embarrassed myself at the event and that my truncated welcome "speech" was beneath me as a CEO. In no way was I serving the role in that moment, and I could have done much better. He was right. I took the feedback with open arms, knowing that he was on my side. Was I cringing? For sure, but I knew he wanted me to succeed. He didn't belittle me—he just told me how I came across. This wasn't a "man up" call—it had nothing to do with gender—it was a "you are way better than this, whatever *better* means for you" call. I received this in the spirit it was delivered and used it to help me improve. And I got better. This was a prime example of why it's so important to find and cultivate mentors who have your back yet also totally hold you to task and to your best performance—or at least a good one. They don't let you fall short and tell you directly when you do.

Here's something else I learned from this experience: being authentic is perhaps more meaningful as a woman than a man. Men are expected to plow through the type of scenario I described and brush it off and it's forgotten. Denying vulnerability is more often rewarded than owning up to it. But there is real strength in letting people see that you recognize where you have fallen short and that you are working to not do it again—to embrace the failing as a growth opportunity. To my mind, the most powerful leaders—male or female—embrace that vulnerability, but men are much less embracing of it in other men. For women, this dichotomy is actually a plus because being more real and vulnerable enables you to forge real and lasting relationships, not just transactional ones.

Here's the thing to remember: when people give you criticism, if they are in a position like Larry Summers, they are delivering it, by and large, with good intentions, not for an ego play. If they are taking the time with you, they care. Otherwise, why would they bother? Years later, Larry is still a confidante and has even coached me in and out of romantic situations. Relationships like this where you can be totally vulnerable with a mentor are so valuable—and they help you be better. Some tearing down may be necessary, but it's like tempering steel.

WHO ARE YOU TO DECIDE YOU'RE NOT WORTHY?

Many powerful men want women to succeed professionally and are willing to help. You just have to ask. I reached out to John Seely Brown around 2010. He ran Xerox Parc (research center), was on the board of Amazon (among others) for twelve years and is one of the most respected innovators of our time. It was a cold, bold outreach. I showed him I respected him, played at his level, and made it clear we had a mutual mission: helping people be smarter and better. I invited him to be a guest on Big Think when he was next in New York. He came on, was impressed with what we do, and wanted to learn more. We spent time together and he got to know better what we do. I thought that he'd be a perfect advisor for Big Think, given his background. But it was a big ask to someone so distinguished and who generally gets paid to do this sort of thing. He actually agreed. More than that, he invested his own money to help us grow.

I've learned along the way to ask for what you want. Be fearless. The only downside is a *no.* As our lead investor constantly said to me: "You don't ask, you don't get." Women sometimes have a tough time asking. Go for it.

Months later, John asked me to be a panelist at the Aspen Institute for a three-day roundtable event he puts on every year with exceptional people from different backgrounds to discuss a particular topic. To say the attendees were intimidating to me, professionally, is an understatement. I did not feel I measured up. While I'd started my own company, I truly was the least qualified to be there based on my overall business experience. All of the people there were rock stars in their particular space—like David Stern—and I was an unknown entity. It was stressful for me from the start. There was a dinner the night before the event began, where we all had to stand up and introduce ourselves and describe what we did. As I heard everybody's background, I thought, *I don't belong here.* Surprisingly (to me), when the dinner actually began, people were really interested to learn about me and Big Think. Despite this, I did still have some of the dreaded imposter syndrome. The next day, participants were seated around the table, discussion was seeded and moderated, and each person was expected to participate. I felt like I was back in HBS, where a large part of your grade was based on participation. Stress! While I knew I didn't *have* to participate, I was aware that I was taking up a seat that could otherwise be filled by someone who would. So, I forced myself to participate.

That feeling I had—of being less valuable and qualified than others at the table—is all too common for women at work. In my case, it turned out not to be true—and I bet that that is the same for most other women too. I will say that the men, for sure, dominated the conversation. But I noticed that men were eager to hear the women's perspective, including mine, as it led to different lines of thought. Despite my intimidation, I contributed. At lunch on one of the days, my then boyfriend and I were looking for a place to sit and there were spots beside David Stern. We went and sat down. This man is brash as can be and no bullshit. Over the course of the lunch, he learned about Big Think, I got his information and several weeks later, when I was back in New York, I asked him to be a guest on Big Think. He came and we chatted after the interview, and he asked me about our financing. Long story short, he became an investor and an unlikely friend to me. He liked our frank conversations. He even coined the term *Digital Goddess,* just for me.

Over the years at Big Think, I've been to countless events when I've questioned why I was invited to attend, much less participate. It did me no good. What's the point? I was and I did. Might as well get on with it and make it worthwhile. Counting myself out as a meaningful "token" contributor—a "diversity admit," as they say—was stupid. It belittles me and those who had the wherewithal to invite me to participate. My notion was, *Well, I'm with this group because they need a young(ish) female to counter all these dudes.* Guess what? That was underestimating the value I could and actually did provide, which led to new insights in an otherwise homogenous context. I was worthy and in fact a differentiator.

Being the only woman in the room can be tough. It can be a lonely place, and it's easy to lose confidence or believe you don't belong. But by being yourself, making bold decisions when appropriate, and embracing others as allies and mentors, you can actually use the situation to your advantage. And it can be really enjoyable to be "different." Often, it makes people want to talk with you and it provides opportunities that don't exist for others. Countless times, I've had the chance to speak with people who are usually difficult to approach or engage with because they are interested in stepping out of the predictable conversations or interactions they're having with businessmen. I provide a glimpse of something different, and I like to think, perhaps even a learning opportunity to expand their horizons and ways of thinking.

REFLECTIONS

◆ Be yourself. Don't dress or act to impress others, make sure you are comfortable and confident.

◆ Assume good intent. Most people are good—don't be needlessly thin-skinned.

◆ Be bold and brash. In the right context, take chances in how you communicate.

CHAPTER 7

AH, THE ROMANCE

The Complicated Dating
Life of a Woman in Power

The setting could not have been more perfect for a fairy-tale proposal: white sands, turquoise blue water, pink sunset. My boyfriend, Michael, unbeknownst to me, had a ring in his pocket when we flew to Thailand over the holidays for a romantic vacation shortly before the launch of Big Think. There was only one problem. By the time we arrived at the designated proposal spot, he was having second thoughts about whether he really wanted to marry a woman who'd spent the entire trip worrying and obsessing over her business and the possible consequences of the "arrest" incident (see Chapter 1). Our relationship didn't survive. The business did.

And that pretty much sums up my love life since I became an entrepreneur.

There are a lot of things I've learned along the way about how *not* to behave in romantic relationships—or in any situation, for that matter—when running a business. I've done so much wrong and treated people in ways I wouldn't want to be treated and likely pushed great people away. Why? Not out of malice but because I was singularly focused—to the detriment of those relationships and others—on building the business.

Here's the tough truth: the qualities needed to be a successful entrepreneur aren't always the qualities that make for a successful relationship. There are appropriate times to be in business mode, and appropriate times to be in romantic/relationship mode, and mostly the two should not mix. They are different entities, with different people, and should be treated as such—each being special. You aren't looking for the same outcome or reward in these relationships. In one, I am looking for love and understanding and the ability to be my truly vulnerable, romantic self. In the other, I'm focused on achieving specific business goals.

No, it's not so easy to play the dating game when you're a female CEO or a CEO at all. Or, actually, anybody responsible for anything beyond yourself. The fact is, you are only responsible for yourself in a relationship and the other person cannot nor should be managed like a business. And that's repeatedly what I've done. Romantic relationships are not transactions; they need to be nurtured in a totally different way.

Which brings me back to that aborted proposal. . . .

Michael (the same guy who told me not to go to the police station) and I started dating in April 2006. Born and raised in Ireland, he had trained and worked as a lawyer there, but one day he saw an ad on an airplane about Columbia Business School and decided he'd rather do that. He uprooted his life, moved to New York, took menial jobs while he attended Columbia, and earned his MBA. He knows sacrifice and hard work. Michael is also a Renaissance man, deeply interested in fashion and style and willing to do pretty much anything I wanted socially, athletically, intellectually, you name it.

Michael was privy to the entire birth of Big Think, from the genesis of the idea, putting together the plans, the fundraising, my quitting Snider to actually starting it and the first almost four years of running it. The man is truly one of the most honorable people I know, and I'm ashamed to say I didn't treat him well much of the time we were together. Not because I didn't want to, but because I was overwhelmed and completely wedded to my job. Perhaps it isn't fair to say, but it seemed I had to be. I felt Big Think literally depended on me. And, in my role as CEO, I didn't have the luxury of ever not being the CEO. When we'd started going out, I was certainly lighter (in spirit). All that changed, or I allowed it to change when I became CEO of Big Think. Small things seemed massive, and I felt that the weight of the world was on my shoulders. Payroll, investors, employees, clients—it all consumed me. I had the now-clearly-wrong conception that I had to "embody" a CEO at all times. I truly felt that if I had that hat, I could never take it off. If I did, things would fall apart. I was stressed all the time and likely not a lot of fun to be around. I eventually learned that nobody, not even the CEO, is critical to a company and that if I am living my life as though I am, things will crumble personally and even professionally. There are times to wear different hats.

As Ev Williams, cofounder and former CEO of Twitter, has said: "Take care of yourself: When you don't sleep, eat crap, don't exercise, and are living off adrenaline for too long, your performance suffers. Your decisions suffer. Your company suffers. Love those close to you: failure of your company is not failure in life. Failure in your relationship is."[1] God, do I know this to be true.

Before Big Think got funded, I needed to keep things inexpensive, so I was living in a shitty little studio apartment in a dodgy part of New York. And it had mice. My parents came to visit me and were like: "You cannot be living there." But I was. Being an entrepreneur is not all rainbows and butterflies.

Just after Big Think got funding, however, I moved into Michael's apartment. He had a penthouse with a wonderful balcony—two bedrooms, two bathrooms, great location. This would be a step up, and a place that would afford us both space as a newly cohabiting couple. Or so I hoped. Just days before I was to move in, Michael was told that there was something structurally wrong in his apartment and he'd have to move immediately into a small one-bedroom several floors below until the construction work was complete. So, I moved into a much tighter situation than I'd expected.

Now, this shouldn't have been a big deal, but I'd never lived with a romantic partner, was working from the apartment quite a bit, and was generally trying to get my bearings about my new position. We didn't have a full-time location for Big Think and everything felt quite unsettled. Not to mention there was someone constantly there with me in the apartment. I'd been used to being alone.

Still, Michael could not have been more gentle. He understood the challenges of making significant professional (and personal) changes. He was committed. Things were going well. I'd been excited about the prospects of this new phase of my life—a new and promising relationship and a new venture! But anxiety got the better of me, and while I was fun to be around much of the time, I was always worried and nervous.

Cut to a few months later, still living in the same situation. Imagine: you just asked this chick to move in with you, but she's started a new venture and is stressed as can be, and then she gets arrested! Making her, well, even more anxious and worried, not only about her reputation, but about how that would affect the company.

There are things more important than your work. Like people you love. But at the time, I wasn't ready to hear or believe that. Over the Christmas holidays that year, Michael and I had planned to go to Thailand, a place he loved. I was excited about the trip and felt that it would be a wonderful respite from all the drama. I hoped to have the legal issues resolved before the trip, so that it was nothing more than a bad memory and possibly a learning experience I could reflect on in the years ahead. Most important, something in my past.

Alas, no.

I learned from my criminal defense attorney that we would not know whether the case was going forward until we came back in the new year. Despite the looming unknown, we decided to go ahead with the trip. I still looked forward to the change of scene but was really not allowing myself to feel anything but anxiety—and that was palpable.

Little did I know that Michael had been planning to propose to me on the trip. I could barely relax for a second. We were in one of the most idyllic places in the world, Krabi Province, Thailand. Crystal-clear water, stunning scenery, perfect weather, and a very, very tense Victoria. I could compartmentalize the work aspect of my life and function seemingly normally in a professional context. In fact, I think I used work calls, which I likely could have avoided at that time of year, to keep a sense of control about my life. What I could not do (well) was function personally or emotionally. On that trip, I went through the motions—swimming, eating, running on the beach, even rock climbing. But the nagging thought of what was going to happen when we returned would not leave me. I was terrified. I neglected the person I was with in favor of an obsession with work and outcomes.

To say that I was not a good travel companion on this trip is an understatement. When we arrived in Thailand, we started off with a bike tour around Bangkok. Cycling in Bangkok is kind of crazy and scary with all the cars and people, but this craziness was a good thing for me. It took my mind off the case for a few moments as I had to focus on staying alive. We went on a tasting tour of a floating market with our bikes and tasted all sorts of delicious food. But whenever my mind was not consumed with staying alive on the busy roads, whenever we stopped to savor experiences and new things, my mind went directly back to the case. I'm sure our travel companions felt sorry for Michael as his somber and moody girlfriend contributed not a whole lot of positivity to the experience. I certainly was not living in the present.

After Bangkok, we flew to an island beach in Krabi. We'd rented a beautiful house, and it was supposed to be a wonderful, relaxing time after months of hard work getting Big Think funded and then putting it into action. I spent most days sullen and snippy. On this "romantic" trip I was uninterested in sex and completely self-absorbed. I sure didn't like me, so I'm certain no one around me did either. It was hardly a surprise when, just after Christmas, in this incredible location, Michael dumped me. Apparently, he'd had a ring in his pocket when we left for Thailand, but on this trip he saw an entirely different Victoria and not only decided he didn't want to marry me, but that he didn't want to be with me at all. Super unhappy, and, yes, self-involved, I called my parents, who offered to pay for a flight back. They understood the pressure and stress I was under and couldn't believe what Michael had done. Had they been with us on the trip, perhaps they'd have seen his side of things. I sure do now, and likely would have done the same as he. He'd reached his limit.

We managed to patch things up before the end of the trip, but I hadn't appreciated the wonderful experience of any of the trip. And I essentially ruined it for him. Lesson to myself: I should have been able to enjoy where I was and who I was with. There are always things to worry about, and my mind jumping to the worst-case scenario is not good for me or the people around me. And as has been said, where you look is where you will go. I know for me, when I focus on something, it tends to happen. At this point I was focusing only on the negative. I should probably have started meditation, but it would take me years to get there.

We arrived home in New York tired and full of emotion after an exhausting, drama-filled trip. Drama-filled, largely because of my fear and erratic emotions surrounding it. Hell, if I were Michael, I'd have been running for the hills. As we walked into our apartment lobby, I felt a rush of panic. I had to go to work the next day, our site was launching in a few days, and the *New York Times* article was coming out on January 7. As much as I didn't want to do it, I did. I went to the mailbox, and there it was: the letter I'd dreaded, telling me the case was going ahead and I'd have to appear in court. You know the rest of the story.

That spring, Michael did propose to me, and we planned to get married in Dublin in April 2009, so his Irish family and my Irish mum and her family could be there, along with my American dad and siblings. It would be in a special location for us. At about this time, the economy had really started to turn, and I was becoming anxious about Big Think's funds. We'd made some sales but I was worried about cash flow (note the theme here: constant worry). A few months later, I had to get a bridge loan from our wonderful lead investor, David Frankel, to keep us going. My mind was truly not on a wedding at all. To be fair to me, I've never had a dream of a white wedding. I think there's a line by Woody Allen about living across the park from Mia Farrow and that being just fine, and while I wouldn't want their relationship, of course, I do think space is important. And, unconventional relationships are just fine with me. Do I want commitment? Yes, but it can be in its own, nontraditional form.

In any case, as 2008 was coming to a close, the economy hit the shits. I just didn't see the reason for an expensive wedding—putting an unnecessary financial burden on us and possibly my dad, who at that point was semiretired. With my cost-conscious CEO hat firmly on my head, I convinced myself it would actually be a gift to both Michael and our families if we eloped.

"Hey, shall we get married this week?" I asked. At first, Michael was a little hesitant, but he agreed. December 9, 2008, I went to Bloomingdales and bought a short dress for the ceremony and had some inappropriate marriage wear: snakeskin Louboutin boots to go along with (a gift from Michael). It was all very rushed. I didn't invite my parents and figured they might actually be relieved, but I knew if I didn't invite Nicholas, my twin brother, he'd be devastated. Winsome, my sister, lived in New York, so I invited her too.

Having a wedding this way was really a lost opportunity. An opportunity for love and a memory between me and my soon-to-be-husband, and also my family. It was a selfish move on my part, and I didn't realize how hurt my parents would be, or my other sister who lives in Atlanta. First, I shouldn't have eloped. But second, if I did, I shouldn't have invited any family to it if I wasn't going to invite them all. My mind was literally elsewhere.

I treated it without respect—a little like a joke. Not reality. Of course, it wasn't.

Friday, December 12, 2008—the day after Bernie Madoff got arrested and the economy was in the shitter—Michael and I went together to city hall. I'd had my hair blown out, wedding day and all. This was my biggest extravagance or investment in the preparation. Hey, big spender! Clearly I was not invested, personally, in the way I should have been. And yes, I took work calls that day and responded to emails. As usual. People in the office didn't even know I was getting married that day, and I'd been at work all of the day before. I thought this was something admirable at the time; now I see that it was quite the opposite.

Winsome and Nicholas met us at the court, as did two of Michael's friends—Mahmoud, a wonderful artist, and David. A motley crew to say the least. Nobody really had any relation to anybody else—outside of family connections. Michael did not have one family member there. It was something like a marriage, but it wasn't what it should have been. Or could have been. It got off on the wrong foot from the start—an afterthought of a wedding, just another sort-of-work day, with something unplanned thrown in.

After the "wedding," we went to a restaurant in Greenwich Village and called our parents. Michael's mother was so sweet and warm. She just expressed happiness for us. I'm sure inside she was sad not to have been there. And, probably upset for her son. Years later, I'm thinking (from her perspective) what kind of a woman/sister/daughter does this to her family or to her fiancé's? That was me, then. I called my parents next. Mum answered the phone and I asked her to get Dad too.

"What is it, Pet?" (*Pet* is an Irish term of endearment.)

"Michael and I just got married!" I blurted out.

There was a pause, and she said, "I'm devastated!" and started crying. "Oh, Pet, why would you do this? It would have been a dream to be there. Dad and I wanted to be there with you. Why did you do this?"

Dad then came on the line, and he was more positive and upbeat, but there was deep sadness in his voice. A happy day? Not so much. Also, I hadn't given the timing fair consideration. The morning after we got married, Michael had planned to go on a shooting trip and had to get up at 5:00 a.m. I'd forced things in pursuit of mammon—business goals. And so, one of the most important experiences of my life was just another day, pretty much. My dad was upset with me for months. He took it hard, and that was tough.

I make decisions quickly as a CEO, as I often need to. But this experience taught me that it's best not to do so in one's personal life. Personal life does deserve a lot more reflection and consideration. Isn't that why we are here? Some people say that you should sleep on things for three nights before making a decision. I'm not so sure it would have helped in this instance, but I do know that I should not be handling my personal life as though it were my job. I hurt people when I behave that way. And I didn't learn all this right away.

I handled the marriage the same way I handled the wedding—without due respect. I was too caught up in making

Big Think work and not letting down our investors, without realizing I was letting down the people closest to me. Even so, Michael was committed to making it work—up to and including having kids. Yes, I also thought, embarrassingly, that kids were something I could cross off my list of achievements. Raising a family was something I needed to do in the same way I needed to raise funds for the company. And I approached it with the same kind of dogged determination.

Unfortunately, my body wasn't cooperating. Given the situation where it was all about work, all the time, I'm sure I was too stressed out to get pregnant. Nature knows the signs of an inhospitable environment, I guess. But not me. So, we went down the IVF route. Twice. Another stressor on us both—have you noticed the theme here? And I was the central stressor.

I started IVF treatments in 2010. IVF is, at minimum, a several-week ordeal, and that's after all the appointments leading up to it (which are manifold). After all the pre-work, so to speak, I started hormone injections, and every morning for twelve or thirteen days I had to wake up at 5:00 a.m. and go to Weill Cornell with dozens of other women to get blood drawn so that they could regulate the meds to take that day. I have tiny veins, so getting blood drawn is an issue. I would drink literally two liters of water beforehand, so my veins were at least somewhat engorged. Sometimes it worked. The nurses were fabulous at keeping me calm, even when they had to stick me numerous times to get even a little blood.

Right after, I'd go straight to work. Didn't want to seem like anything was amiss! Not this CEO! Not now, not ever.

Perception mattered intensely. Being the first in and the last out, somehow, was key. The concept of love for myself and for my husband, at this time when we were trying to create new life, eluded me.

Every evening during this period, I was giving myself injections in the thigh. Not exactly the stuff of romance—and especially not with someone who was still talking business all the time. I didn't have an off switch. Or a romance switch. At some point in the cycle, Michael had to go in and "deposit" to fertilize the egg. Then, I believe a day and a half before egg retrieval, you have to get a timed "trigger" shot so the eggs are primed for removal. Miss this window and you miss your shot. Like Hamilton, I wasn't throwing away my shot! Each woman is scheduled within a very short time frame, and the doctor follows that time to a T. My time was 10:00 p.m. I was worried I'd not get it right, as there was just one needle with the meds, so I paid a nurse to do it. Thing is, I lost the shot along the way. Desperately, I called my doctor to get a new one. Time was running out! This should have been a sacred moment, but we approached it with panic, which I'd created. I'd been dealing with work stuff all day, not the way more important thing at hand. By the time we made it to the nurse's home, we were frazzled. She was already in her pajamas, but kindly welcomed us in—likely she'd seen this many times before. We had made it just in time. Unlike the business world, where JIT (just-in-time) delivery is a good thing, when it's your life, it's best not to mess around that way.

The next step was egg retrieval—not a comfortable procedure and also intricately timed. Each woman is given a specific slot based on the time of her trigger shot. As it happened, this was the day of the New York City Marathon, and we had to go from the Upper West to the Upper East right as the race was taking place. No easy shakes. We ended up having to walk/run a lot of the way. In retrospect, it was a funny scene—all these runners streaming through the city and me, thirteen days into a major hormone treatment, with ovaries (we hoped) brimming with eggs, fighting against the tide to get to my appointment on time. Perhaps it was an apt metaphor for the way I was approaching parenthood. It was certainly not comfortable.

The retrieval ensued and was successful. We had a bunch of viable embryos. Good results! Next came the implantation. The first cycle didn't work. Nor the second. Quite honestly, I don't think my body was relaxed enough to be receptive.

After all these ups and downs in our marriage, largely caused by me, it's no wonder things fell apart. In the spring of 2011, it was clear that I was a mess. I was essentially avoiding the marriage, spending little time at home, and while we were each other's most trusted confidants, the romance wasn't there. I'd invested so much in the business and so little in the most important thing in my life, the people I loved.

Here's the thing, though: Michael and I remain very close, even after our divorce. Why? Despite my many foibles, I am me, whoever "me" is in the moment. I'm trusted and loved even at my worst because I let people in—those who are close to me. Romantic partners especially. Michael has been my go-to guy for stylin' my apartments ever since. He's helped me over and over. He's so nonjudgmental, and he gets me as a person because I was open with him from the get-go. He saw that in me. When shit is getting real at work, I may not be my badass fun self as I want to be in romantic relationships, but I'm always genuine.

DON'T OVERCOMPENSATE

Sometimes, you gotta go against the grain to grow. To put yourself in a different scenario than you have experienced before. In business or in personal matters, it's a good thing. Working new angles provides new scenarios. And those are sometimes what it takes to help you (personally) and the business morph to something spectacular. Change drives growth. Hard change may drive it more. That said, it's easy to overcompensate, as I learned after my breakup with Michael.

I certainly went for a change with my post-divorce relationship. I chose the absolute opposite of what I'd had personally and professionally, up to that point. I put myself in a dating scenario where I had almost no control. And, for some time, that was intoxicating. I learned from it. And . . . I won't do it again.

Here's how it went down. After the split, I'd been dating a little bit and had some fun here and there, but my mind was not on anything serious. One day, my sister invited me to a Broadway show—a three-play feature benefitting a board she was on. I wasn't in the mood to go, and I tried to cancel that afternoon, but Winsome said: "I could have asked anybody, and I asked you. You cannot say no."

Begrudgingly, I went. The last of the three plays, written by Woody Allen and directed by John Turturro, was a well-performed, funny piece. I recognized a couple actors from eighties sitcoms and movies I'd seen as a kid. When it was over, I was ready to go home. Nope! Winsome said, "There's an after-party." Big sisters can be bossy. So I went to the party, wearing gray, high-heeled Mary Jane shoes, a black-and-gray-striped dress, a tired attitude, and a not-in-the-mood face.

Picture a buffet. Picture mounds of sushi. Hello, Times Square tourist trap with a bunch of people who don't want to be there. Especially the actors, who were forced to attend. Me, a definite non-actor, standing in the corner. Winsome being her usual warm, engaging self, mingling and bringing out the best in others. Then—flashback to age twelve!—the eighties movies star struck up a conversation with me. Soon, his friend the sitcom actor joined as well. And my charming sister.

As the four of us were standing there talking, I was like, WTF. Time to skedaddle. Two famous actors, two sisters, a giant mound of sushi, Times Square. All of these were *no's* to me. Get me the fuck out. But Winsome was telling them about me and Big Think, so I couldn't just leave. I could tell there was at least a glimmer of interest from them both in me physically. I was more interested in the film guy, Tom, and the TV guy knew it, so he moved away slightly. I later learned that they worked it out between themselves and Tom got to call me. Bro code.

Long story short, Tom and I got involved. He was impressed with my good manners, HBS degree, Big Think, my interest in conversation, and my unphased attitude to his fame. I was having a ball. Going from a rather staid relationship to this was a complete 180. I probably should have realized that things that burn so bright at the start tend to flame out. And it did, almost three years later.

Over the course of that relationship I learned that I would (at that time) put up with inappropriate behavior in service of passion. I won't do it again. I had no control over his where-abouts, and not even communication from him. He'd disappear for months then show up and assume I still wanted to be with him. By my own choice, I was in a constantly on-again-off-again relationship and never really knew where I stood. He'd embarrass me by showing up stoned for business-related social functions and freak out if he wasn't the center of attention. The Hollywood world was not something I was used to. It was up and down—extreme highs and lows all the time. No stability. I think I tolerated it because I was the person trying to control everything at Big Think, and this was a scenario where I had control of nothing. Over the three years we dated, we were on and off but the passion never left.

In 2013, I began the process of freezing my eggs. Solo. When you are with someone and you are freezing eggs, it's most likely time to think again. I guess I was the CEO of my own body too. It felt good to be creating options for myself. I know many other women in business—confronting the reality that their fertile years are also the years when they are trying to build their careers—feel the same. As a *New York Times* article in March 2018 points out, egg freezing has grown sharply over the past decade.[2] In 2009, just a few hundred women underwent the procedure, compared to 6,207 women in 2015 (according to the Society of Assisted Reproductive Technology). Some Silicon Valley companies even pay for their employees to do it. This all seems like good news—options are good, right? But the vast majority of women who have frozen their eggs have never had them thawed, which is the first step toward actually creating a baby.

Tom was going to take me to the retrieval for the egg freezing, but of course at the last minute he decided to go to Los Angeles instead, so yet again I was let down and left alone. For some reason the retrieval for the egg freezing was far worse than it had been for IVF. I was up in the middle of the night wondering if I should go to the hospital as it felt like hot pokers in my abdomen. I didn't even receive a call to ask if I was okay.

Of course, my relationship with Tom wasn't all bad—there were times when we got along wonderfully and really enjoyed being around each other. But those times didn't last long. I should have broken up with him long before I did. I think I was addicted to trying to win his favor. Had we had some of our experts on narcissism on Big Think earlier, I might well have got out sooner. Some of the telltale signs of narcissists I've learned since then include: frequent lying and exaggerating, rarely admitting flaws and becoming highly aggressive when criticized, false image projection (Tom would look in the mirror and say, "I'm looking better every day"), rule breaking, emotional invalidation, and manipulation. I learned that I need to recognize these in the future and move on from them quickly.

Tom continually made me feel that I was the cause of all the arguments and problems. He'd pick fights, blame me, and then, as narcissists do, try to woo me back. Of course, it worked. Please note: It's unwise to date narcissists, and it's also unwise to work with them. However, it's somewhat hard to spot them because their initial MO is total charm.

It all came to a head at a wedding, sometime early in 2014. One of Tom's friends, a successful business guy, was marrying a young, hot model. It was officiated by a forty-ish, handsome rabbi. Tom was in one of his moods that evening, and I felt alone. I remember calling my brother and telling him I wanted to leave. When I returned from the call, I bumped into the rabbi, and he and I began to talk. I was literally the only shiksa in the room. Something seemed amiss with me, he observed. I seemed unhappy. He gave me his contact information and said to come and see him any time. And I did. We had coffee a couple weeks later in New York. He asked me some hard questions about the relationship and without doing so directly, was coaching me out. We met many times over the next few months.

Sometimes the best advice comes from people with no experience of you, who just observe the reality as it is. And in this case, the reality was good for neither Tom nor me. But I'm loyal to a fault and don't give up. Sometimes giving up is the right thing to do! I finally ended it a few months later. And yes, the rabbi and I got together after Tom and I broke up. Briefly. We're still friends.

Post-Tom, I went a little nuts. Having been in a marriage, then a three-year relationship, I decided, to heck with it! It's time to have fun. So fun I had with, among others, a hot Brazilian, former world-class squash player who lived in Miami. The interesting thing about almost all my flings was that my directness was initially appealing to the fellow, and then perhaps a turnoff. As my sister said to me, it's important to keep business out of the bedroom. I am always problem-solving for myself and others. There's a time and a place, and it isn't in romance.

WHEN YOU HAVE TO TALK YOURSELF INTO SOMETHING, YOU'RE PROBABLY BETTER OFF OUT OF IT

Next, I went online. Even though it seemed pretty unappealing, I'm open to change and also to opportunity, so I gave it a go. After all, I was the Digital Goddess, right? When I first met Alex, I didn't think we were a match and kept putting off meeting him, but he was persistent. Over the course of the next few weeks, I talked myself into dating him. "This is a nice, Midwestern guy. He will be kind," I told myself. We went on a number of dates and he grew on me. Sort of. He was funny and charming and really seemed to care about me. Before I knew it, I'd invited him on vacation with me, and he'd asked me to move in. After just a couple months of dating. I should have seen the red flags. Things that seem too good to be true mostly are. But I plowed on, regardless, and moved into his West Village sixth-floor walkup. Thing is, even though we'd been dating for some time, he traveled so much that I never really spent that much time with him. And, as he got to know me, the things that he initially thought were so appealing actually were my downfall.

Being a strong CEO on paper is attractive, dealing with it up close and personal in close quarters, maybe not so much. Apparently "my tone" was an issue. Also, my directness. Again, qualities that are good in business, but not always welcome in a relationship. We moved again into a jointly leased apartment, and I may as well have moved in alone. As the months went by, he was traveling all the time, and any time he could, would be going home to his mother for long periods of time. Before the year was out, we were both putting the brakes on our relationship. Still, my "no quitter" business attitude kicked in and I was not willing to give up.

In December, I happened to have coffee with Larry Summers and he, in his brilliant way, walked me through the decision I needed to make.

L: "Victoria, you're in your early forties, right?"

V: "Yes."

L: "This isn't your first relationship, right?"

V: "No."

L: "Well, is this a situation you want to keep going? You haven't been with this person very long at all. It's not like a divorce, you don't have kids. Something that is central to who you are, your directness, is, in the context of this relationship, a negative for him. Do you have the information you need?"

V: "Yes."

I shouldn't have needed such a brilliant business strategist to help me make such an obvious decision. This was one moment when putting on my CEO hat would have helped my personal life. But I was grateful to Larry for the push. A week or so later,

I came home to Alex sitting on the couch in the dark, with his boots and coat on, telling me he had moved into a hotel. We sorted through the lease, but things were over and done. There were key lessons to learn here, most notably to see the signs and trust your gut. Don't force things and, if you do go down the wrong path, don't keep investing more in the hopes of making things better. The sunk costs fallacy can be as dangerous in relationships as it is in business. Get out. Had I not been so focused on business, that relationship likely wouldn't have even gotten off the ground.

Since then, I think the entrepreneurial spirit has certainly influenced my romantic life. I am open to possibility. I am still optimistic. I don't regret any of my romantic experiences as they have helped me grow. And I've had fun along the way—and continue to do so.

REFLECTIONS

◆ Don't be CEO of your romance. Romantic partnerships deserve their own space and investment; separate business and personal relationships.

◆ Don't date (or hire) narcissists. While initially intoxicating, narcissists will eventually bring you down emotionally and psychologically.

◆ Mitigate risk. Taking risks is appropriate for your role as an entrepreneur. Risky relationships are not worth it.

◆ There is always another. Don't get stuck in a situation because you think it's your only shot.

CHAPTER 8

YOUR OTHER MARRIAGE

How Not to Divorce
Your Business Partner

Sometimes I think my relationship with Peter, my cofounder, is closer than a marriage. In fact, he likes to call me his "daytime wife" (not that he has a nighttime wife, being gay). We really are in it for the long haul, for richer or for poorer, for better and for worse. "Better" is the creative partnership we share, the way we can finish each other's sentences and execute on our company's mission. "Worse," in our case, were some pretty dark times . . . but more on that in a moment.

When you commit to a business partner, it's more than just business. Your success becomes dependent on your partner's success, and vice versa. It can easily become the most important relationship in your life, to the detriment of other relationships. And yet there is little guidance available for improving this critical partnership in the way you might work on improving a marriage. I want to share the lessons I've learned about what you can do (and not do) to keep this "other marriage" out of the divorce courts.

For starters, it's imperative that business partners have different roles, and they respect them—like the Woz and Jobs dynamic. I think I'm creative, but I'm not as creative as Peter. I know I'm more decisive than Peter. For whatever reason, I command authority and I'm able to make decisions quickly and not look back. Peter is the ultimate optimist, while I am the ultimate pragmatist. These things are complementary, they can also be a challenge in working relationships.

Over time, we figured out our roles. And it clicked. While we are equal partners in the business, I'm the decision-maker at Big Think. It wasn't always that way. Initially there were some conflicts and misunderstandings, but over time it became clear how our roles needed to be different. Staff always came to me when they had issues and looked to me to resolve things. In a sense, it's calming for both of us to know where the buck stops. Yes, we talk about all major decisions, but everybody in the company knows that ultimately, I decide. While it's a lot of pressure for me, it's essential to know how things work. Early on, people didn't really know who had the ultimate authority and final word. It was confusing to the staff and led to disagreements. It's just far more simple and effective if everyone knows where things stand. Am I always right? Not even close. I've made so many errors along the way—cost us business, lost clients, lost people—but that's normal. The role of the CEO is to make decisions, even if they turn out to be wrong.

Peter is a visionary. Many of the products and proposals that have been successful at Big Think have been his brainchildren. Initially, I felt bad that I didn't have the same sort of insight into patterns and trends on the horizon. But I've come to realize that it's actually a good thing that I am not as talented as him in that regard. When he brings a creative idea to me and we agree to pursue it, it's my job to execute on it. Does he help in that process? Absolutely, but we know when boundaries need to be put into place and our respective roles enacted.

Big Thinkers Say . . .

As celebrated psychotherapist Esther Perel told a live audience at NeueHouse for a Big Think event in 2017, "business couples" can thrive in much the same way successful marriages do.[1] How? There needs to be a foundation of respect. There also needs to be the ability and desire to address conflict as soon as it occurs and the willingness to take responsibility for your behavior and actions and mistakes. Last, understanding where you are complementary allows differences to make for a stronger partnership. "Complementarity is the possibility for each person to be who they are. So complementarity is your partner allowing

> you to be who you are at your best without having to try to do that which you can learn but will never be your second nature."[2]

NAVIGATING CONFLICT

There are times when partners, in any context, need a break from each other. This is especially true after big fights, and Peter and I have had plenty—usually reflecting our different sensibilities. As I said, our strengths are mostly complementary, but that doesn't mean they don't clash.

Here's just one example: we were putting together an important VIP event that was to be held at my sister's house. Peter and I were traveling together at the time and got into a huge and volatile fight. Tensions had been brewing about the event. I thought it was unrealistic to have the incredible guest list Peter wanted and have it fully catered and cleaned up seamlessly for free. Here was an example of my negativity and practicality coming up against his belief that anything is possible. It was a stupid fight, but one of our most intense. Often it's the small issues that have led to our biggest conflicts. We tend to get through the more serious issues better. I can't remember exactly what was said, but I had a sense that things would never be the same between us again. Over pretty much nothing.

We both eventually retreated and avoided each other for the remainder of the trip. It was very uncomfortable. The next day we had to make our way through very winding roads to the airport. We'd rented a car and I was the driver. Peter put his headphones on so there was no discussion. I felt anxious, as is my way. He seemed pretty chill, but still quietly seething. We arrived at the airport, returned the car, and made our way separately into the terminal. From that point on, we were on the same trip but not traveling together. We didn't communicate and he sat away from me on the plane.

The whole trip back, I was anxious. How would this be restored? Was he going to leave? My mind, as it often does, went to the worst possible outcome. Back in New York City, he got off the plane and didn't look back. He got into a taxi and went home, and I did the same. We resolved the fight by literally just getting on with our jobs—the event was happening, and we needed to put it together. While emotions were raw, diving in and focusing on the issue at hand was the solution, rather than rehashing. Sometimes you just have to walk away from each other, and take a break, as in any relationship.

I asked myself, What's more important, the relationship or the fight? I think this is a critical question to ask yourself in the midst of whatever fight you are having, to give yourself and the other person space to cool off and be level-headed. It's also important to know the role you usually play in the resolution of fights. I tend to be a peacemaker, the more balanced one. I'm not a hothead and I crave resolution. In the majority of fights I'm in, I tend to extend the olive branch as I want to preserve relationships. It's also important to know how the other person usually reacts, and what he or she needs to get past the argument and be in a better place than before. It's important that one person offers the olive branch, but the other person still has to accept it. Peter is good at burying the hatchet and moving on once the situation is addressed.

In this particular example, I knew that it would be up to me to resolve the conflict by apologizing, even if I didn't feel that I was in the wrong. I also had a sense it was best not to do it immediately. Oftentimes, we can get past the impasse with time and distance. This has been a strategy Peter and I have employed repeatedly. In such instances, you may simply need to distance yourself from your cofounder.

For instance, sometimes when I get too relentlessly practical, it pisses Peter off. Being around the same person with the same stresses day after day can take a toll. Sometimes you just need to not see each other for a while. When resolving fights with Peter, I try to ask myself, What is it really that he does not want to go beyond? What is the actual boundary here?

Sometimes things get really serious in partnerships, and the way you handle it will affect the person, the company, and your relationship irreversibly. I've had two such situations with Peter. In December 2007, we both had a ton of things going on in our lives. I was still dealing with the arrest and waiting to see what would happen next. Peter was suddenly very ill and getting worse on a daily basis. That was enough in our personal lives alone, but we were also one month away from launching Big Think.

....

Sometimes things get really serious in partnerships, and the way you handle it will affect the person, the company, and your relationship irreversibly.

....

These were the days when we were literally working in a storage closet, sitting back to back in a space of about twenty square feet. Spending every day in this confined space with Peter, I knew something was off. He was clearly very unwell and trying to power through it. Symptoms I observed or he told me about included coughing, diarrhea, constant sweating. Whoa. He needed to go to the doctor. One afternoon, we were sitting in our little cubicle and it was nearing the end of the day. He got a call and afterward asked me to come and chat with him. He was calm but clear it was urgent.

We met in our shared conference room, he closed the door, and matter-of-factly told me he'd tested positive for HIV. I was shocked. I immediately went to hug him, and he burst into tears. It was one of the most upsetting moments of my life, and of course, even more so his. I did my best to be comforting. There was nothing to say except that I was there for him. We hugged for some time and I told him things would be okay, and we'd figure it out together. I was so worried about his physical and also mental health. People handle diagnoses differently, and I was concerned that this might just catalyze a free-for-all, where life meant a whole lot less to him so he may as well say fuck it and behave recklessly. He went home and took a few days to be alone with his new reality. I was constantly calling him to make sure he was okay and check on his mind-set. This is one point in time where it was clear that our friendship was far more important than whatever happened to Big Think.

How you treat your partner about things affecting life outside of the office is almost as important as how you treat him or her about the things going on in it. That's how you build trust. Empathy is essential, as is nonjudgmental behavior. We all make mistakes, and life throws us all curveballs. The critical thing is how we deal with them. My sister Winsome had a friend who contracted HIV in the eighties and it had gone to full-blown AIDS. In 2007, he was still alive—a rarity at that time—so I called her and asked her to put her friend in touch with Peter. That's how Peter got his HIV doctor and began the drug cocktail that keeps him largely symptom-free. These days, there is another drug, PrEP (pre-exposure prophylaxis), that can prevent transmission. After a few days of reflection and telling his family, Peter was back at Big Think. I was impressed by and proud of how he dealt with it—his openness and willingness to discuss his fears. I know the temptation would be to hide his diagnosis but he was clear with those close to him. While the diagnosis was in no way a good thing, it did, I feel, lead to some positive behavior changes. He matured very quickly and while he can still be a hothead and get very angry, he became calmer and more reflective. And he was more focused than ever on Big Think. He was handling the reality with dignity and strength and optimism—the same way he has dealt with many of the challenges that came our way.

WHEN COFOUNDERS BECOME CODEPENDENT

It wasn't all roses for the next six years. In 2013, I was forced to confront and deal with a reality I really didn't want to be true. Peter was addicted to crystal meth. I started to notice some erratic behavior. He was coming in to work late, and seemed manic, at times. His eyes were a little too intensely focused, his jaw clenched, and he was displaying some aggressive behavior. Additionally, he would disappear for days at a time and then arrive midway through a project that the entire staff had agreed upon and at the last minute try to insert himself and change everything.

The staff was also beginning to notice that this wasn't just Peter's typical creative behavior, it was off the rails. His mood was erratic, and he seemed to explode at little things—sending people emails at odd hours, not responding for days and then sending a flurry of emails requesting people do things that really didn't make sense.

I didn't want to confront the situation. Usually, I'm totally direct, but in this instance I wanted to deny it. We'd been having a rough go with business not being great, and it was a situation that I compartmentalized when I shouldn't have. There are times in partnerships when it makes sense to compartmentalize in order to push things forward, and other times when a situation needs to be addressed immediately.

The moment came when I could no longer avoid it. Not for me, not for the company, not for the staff, and most of all, not for Peter. At the time, we had about twenty employees. We were hosting an event at the Norwood Club in New York City to drum up business for our corporate licensing product, Big Think Edge. The prior evening, starting around 11:00 p.m., frantic emails from Peter began circulating to the staff—making last-minute changes to the program and demanding a lot of additional work and preparation. He had been slightly absent during the entire preparation, because he was deep in the throes of the addiction. If I'm truly honest with myself, I knew he was on drugs; I just didn't know what kind. This was a clear example of my enabling Peter—which is often a pattern in close relationships, even business ones. In psychological terms, it's called being codependent.

Codependency is pervasive in all sorts of relationships. And, I've found, it's critical to identify quickly and change behavior. One of the key symptoms of it is becoming emotionally and/or psychologically dependent on someone. Usually there is someone in the relationship who needs/demands more support or attention because of something major going on in his or her life—whether it be illness, addiction, or another such crisis. It's clear, in hindsight, that my sweeping things under the carpet for Peter, for myself, and for anybody in his orbit had actually facilitated some of his completely inappropriate behavior by allowing and excusing it and pretending it didn't exist. Denial is a huge part of codependency, and so is putting up with bad behavior and even covering for the person. Well, eventually I was forced to confront both my codependency and Peter's addiction. Peter called me late the night before our event to vehemently complain about how things were being handled. It wasn't good. And yet, I still didn't take appropriate measures. I was walking on eggshells. Our team was calling me and emailing me and expressing huge concern not just for themselves but for him. They were worried the event would be a flop and didn't want him there.

Instead of taking action and telling him not to come, I found it easier to ignore it and forge ahead. The next day I played multiple roles—host, moderator, and deflector-in-chief. I was pretending to myself and others that Peter was okay, and everybody could tell that he was not. We had a fine program, featuring business leaders including David Westin and Tom Glocer. I was really nervous for Peter to arrive. I wasn't sure which Peter we would get: the super intelligent, charming one, or the guy who'd been angry, aggressive, absent, virtually foaming at the mouth. We got the latter, without the foam. It was not a productive event. Not a total loss, but bad for the morale of the company and team. I seemed weak. I was not being a leader in that moment, or the weeks leading up to it. The experts we'd invited to speak expressed concern to me about Peter. I continued to cover for him. He was my partner, and I didn't want him to be harmed, but the harm of avoiding it was far worse.

Big Thinkers Say . . .

Making tough decisions is a CEO's job. My mentor Larry Summers taught a Big Think Edge masterclass on how to make tough decisions, in which he points out that the core challenge is to separate what you would like to be true from what in fact is true. "For practical purposes, for decision makers, if you're deciding whether to introduce a new product, or you're deciding whether to create a new division of your company, or you're deciding the right person to hire—for those kinds of decisions, it's important to understand what is true and to understand how the world works so that you can judge the consequences of alternative courses of action as accurately as possible. And what's essential is not to confuse what one would like to be true with what, in fact, is true."[3] Negotiating truth, Larry says, is the enemy of good decision-making. In the Peter situation, for months, I had failed on this count, to the detriment of both him and the company.

The day after the event, every person on the staff told me that they had a huge issue with Peter and wouldn't stay if he was a part of the regular team. He could not be in a manage-rial role or we'd lose our staff. Nobody wanted to report to him, and they didn't want to be given assignments by him. Shit had hit the skids. I had been hoping that I was wrong but was actually living a lie by looking the other way. It was real. Peter was a drug addict. It was past time to act. I wanted him to get help and kick the habit. I also had a fiduciary responsibility to protect the company and our people. Protecting the company trumps any loyalty you have to your business partner. In this instance, I had to wear two separate hats, CEO and friend. It was the most difficult time of our partnership.

You cannot just be nice in this kind of crisis; you need to be effective. And while it can seem harsh to be totally direct, sometimes it must be done, and forcefully. You can do it respectfully, but you must get it done. Separately, you can be a friend and help in that regard. The relationship of a business partner sometimes needs to just be professional for the sake of the company.

I'd waited too long. This was my friend, my business partner, literally the most important relationship in my life at the time, and he was a mess. I told Peter what the staff had said and what I must do. He was not happy at all—totally in denial. I think he knew I was aware of what was going and was a little incredulous I'd waited so long. I let him know that he would not be allowed to work from the office in the near future at least, until he cleaned himself up. Additionally, nobody was to report to him, and he couldn't give the staff assignments. Everything had to come through me. Believe me, this was not something I wanted to take on. He was angry and threatened to sue. He was at rock bottom. I was deeply concerned that having him out of the office would catalyze him to spiral further out of control. And, for a time, it did. But I had to act. He disappeared for a while and was very angry with me. Excising Peter from the business was one of the hardest things I've had to do personally and professionally. But I had to. I literally didn't have a choice as the CEO of the company.

With Peter gone—and me not knowing what he was doing on a day-to-day basis—I needed help. I couldn't run Big Think alone. And I didn't want Peter to feel that there was no path back for him. So I reached out, and finally we connected. He was still extremely angry but did want the company to thrive and survive. It was still his baby. I knew that including him in the decision about who we brought on to help me during this period (and beyond) would be important. He suggested his former college roommate Roger, who became our COO. Seeking Peter's advice and keeping him in the loop played a critical part in his recovery. It calmed him to know that his friend was a part of the company.

When you have been extremely open with someone for years and have come to love that person, even the toughest situations can be worked through if both parties have the right motivation and are invested in a positive outcome. Step back and ask yourself, what are we really working toward here? In this case, it was the success of the company. Roger was very qualified and in some ways, hiring him served as the aforementioned olive branch. Peter could see he wasn't being pushed out. We just wanted him to get better.

This was an important time for Peter too. He was grappling with the fact that his behavior had consequences and if he didn't change it, he would not only be harming himself physically, but professionally too. It took some time, but he got it together. And came back. Better and stronger than ever. He was more committed to Big Think than I had seen in years. I think always allowing for the possibility of redemption is a huge part of successful partnerships. At least for me. It builds confidence to know that you can fail—even badly—and if you rectify things, there is a still a possibility (though not a guarantee) of a new path forward, together. This trust has been extended to me, too, by Peter when I have had missteps (which you will read more about in the next chapter).

Here are the key things I've discovered about partnerships. We can only control ourselves, and to some extent the environment. Nothing else. Additionally, it's not an all-or-nothing scenario and shouldn't be approached as such. Situations change and being flexible is important. I'm sure a lot of people would not have allowed Peter to come back. I didn't see things that way. I allowed for the opportunity that he would change and even grow from the experience, and he did. I think being flexible and, more important, empathetic, in business partnerships is essential. Sometimes you must act, but it doesn't mean anything needs to be permanent. And good can come from really difficult times and experiences.

Choosing a business partner is a crucial process and getting it wrong can produce disastrous results. You're going to have to spend a ton of time with this person, and if you're not enjoying it then it's not worth it. You also need to ensure that you have what it takes between you to run a business successfully. Finally, when you have met a good business partner, you'll need to decide when is the time to stand by that person and when you need to cut and run. All of this can make you seem slightly ruthless, but it is not. As my father would say to me, "It's no gift to hang a man slowly." Situations change in every partnership, and how you relate must change, too, for the best outcome. Understanding and acting as if you are committed to each other's well-being, no matter what, is the objective. And, even in times of deep uncertainty and actual turmoil, if you have created this fundamental reality, the relationship will survive long after whatever business issues you've been working on.

REFLECTIONS

- Cultivate long lasting relationships. Enduring relationships bring real meaning to your professional life.

- Define your role. Each partner needs a clearly defined role—they may need time to evolve.

- Grow from hardship. Difficult situations can strengthen rather than tear down partnerships.

- Avoid codependency. The only thing you can control is yourself. Set boundaries and stick to them.

CHAPTER 9

DON'T PANIC!

Running a Start-up without Having a Breakdown

"I'm having a stroke."

It seemed crazy—I was in my early forties, fit, and healthy. And yet all the signs seemed to be telling me I needed to get myself to a hospital right away. I'd been having lunch with the global head of innovation at Pfizer, a very important client, when I began to feel "off," to say the least. I felt shaky and unstable—like I'd topple over if I were to stand up.

Excusing myself, I hastily said goodbye, got myself into a cab, and went straight to Mount Sinai Medical Center. Arriving at the hospital, I caused quite a scene, shouting that I was having a stroke. The professionals sprang into action, rushing me to the ER and into immediate triage, with six doctors gathered around me.

Many hours and tests later, turns out it was a panic attack. I felt foolish, but also frightened—was I having a breakdown? Had the stress of feeling so responsible for the company and our investors' money finally gotten the better of me?

Mental health is a topic that's often left out of the start-up conversation. But it shouldn't be. Stress and anxiety are familiar states to most founders, and we rarely speak openly about how we deal with them. In my time as a CEO, I've battled chronic anxiety and worse. Leading up to the full-on panic attack, I had a series of mini-breakdowns, including a board meeting where I almost passed out. I've had to come to grips with the fact that I can't control everything and must find strategies for managing my own mind in the midst of turmoil. I've begun to learn how to give myself a break and take care of my mental health.

I've always had deep-seated insecurities about letting people down. When it came to Big Think, I felt the weight of the world on my shoulders as I struggled to come to terms with the expectations that come from securing investments. People had invested with free will and absolutely knew the risks of putting their money in a start-up, but I couldn't shake the feeling that they had invested in me and I was personally responsible for every penny they put in. I also thought Big Think must have a "big" and successful exit and if we didn't, they would feel that I'd duped them somehow, or at least let them down.

It was a constant refrain in my head—How will I have a successful exit? We'd managed to raise money at a decent valuation along the way, and that meant that a "successful" exit would have to be well beyond the valuation at which the investors put their money in. It's a double-edged sword—you want a high valuation, but the higher it is, the more the business has to sell for in order to achieve a successful exit.

As time marched on and reality kicked in, my expectations recalibrated, and I just wanted to find at least an exit where investors would at least get their money back. I felt paralyzed with anxiety. My mind played out the worst-case scenario over and over. Typically, I kept this to myself, sharing my worries only sometimes with Peter, but never fully revealing the extent of my trauma. It was hard to experience any sense of lightness or joy, and it was affecting me physically too. I started to have vertigo and anxiety when traveling in cars and planes, always imagining getting into a crash. I was no longer all that fun to be around. I wasn't experiencing joy or happiness, I was never present in the moment, and I was constantly living in fear.

It was no way to live. When positive opportunities presented themselves, I would examine them from the perspective of how they might fail instead of how they could benefit me and the company. It's likely that trauma from earlier parts of my life contributed to this, including my arrest. It's something I could have gotten over way sooner with some help, which I eventually got. People who are living lives of pressure often need external help. It's the rare few who don't. Getting outside of yourself is critical, and you are often unable to do that alone. And it's important to note, help is not a one-time thing. For mental stability, it needs to be ongoing.

Peter and I were in San Francisco in the late spring of 2016, and I was falling into a downward mental spiral. Though I do tend to plan for the worst and hope for the best, as the cliché goes, at this point in my life I could see only doom. Nine years of running the business, along with a whole bunch of personal things going wrong—including the breakup of a marriage, a significant relationship ending, and the death of my mother—had led me close to the breaking point. I say close, because I didn't quite break. I got help, and I truly thank Peter for insisting on it.

I remember exactly how and when it happened. We were sitting in Yerba Buena Gardens having a drink after a day of meetings. As usual, I was talking about our cash flow and how we were soon to be in a terrible predicament. Like a broken record, I started working through what we would need to do, step by step, in terms of layoffs. This was something I'd been doing for months. Now, I unleashed all my fears—not something I encourage, because it brings others down too.

"Here's how bad it is," I declared to Peter. "I'm afraid the investors are going to be really upset with how we've managed this company. They are not going to be supportive, and they are likely going to sue us for mismanagement." I laid out the absolute worst-case scenario, with no appreciation of how supportive our investors had been over the years, and how they valued what we had created and continued to create on a shoestring budget. I was getting even more anxious, and I could see I was actually getting to Peter too. He looked downtrodden.

Finally, he said to me, "If we are going to get sued, and the investors are going to hate us, why are we doing this?" It was a moment where I asked myself, *WTF am I doing?* What am I putting myself and those around me through? While Peter was the one most immediately affected by my anxiety, I had put others around me through it too—including my family and friends. I was spiraling and could focus on nothing else.

Peter and I then had a very tough and real conversation. He said he couldn't continue to work with me as I was, and that I needed help. He told me I was bringing people around me down and it wasn't okay. Most of all, I had very little optimism, despite being an optimist at heart. Yes, I'm a realist but, as is evident by what I've done with Big Think and inspired those around me to do for twelve years, I am an optimist. At that moment, however, it was clear I'd lost sight of that positive outlook. Things had to change, for my own mental well-being and the well-being of those around me.

It was one of the hardest moments in my life. I had to act. And, if there's one thing I know, it's how to keep on moving, set goals, and work to get results. In this case, the goal was to start creating mental stability and to get my head in a sound place. I remember sitting at the table with Peter and thinking, Victoria, right now you need to recognize that something is seriously off with you. Enough denial. You are ruining your life and making the lives of others around you less happy. Time to take ownership and make changes. Now.

So, I told Peter I was going to get help. It's not like I couldn't function on a day-to-day basis—I was still CEO, still leading the company, and everyone knew I was in charge. I just wasn't in full charge of my own mind. But what to do? I was already meeting with a therapist, Amanda, here and there. She has been super helpful over the years, almost like a mother figure after my mum died and I went through divorce and other challenges. I didn't want to admit I really needed more or different help than she could provide at that moment.

I called her and told her where things were. And then, hesitantly, I said, "I hate to say this, but it may be time that I tried some medication." Truly, it was the last thing I wanted to do. I had a self-conceived notion (definitely not imparted by my parents) that any medication for depression or anxiety was bad, a sign of weakness. I thought anyone who believed they needed meds, including me, should just get a grip on herself and put on her big-girl pants. But that was the thinking of someone who had never experienced serious anxiety that was cascading into depression or been around anyone truly suffering from it.

Amanda comforted me and said she thought I could be right. Of course she wasn't going to push me in one direction or the other. She suggested a few psychiatrists I could speak with. Alas, all of them were busy for months ahead, and I couldn't wait. I had been through some tumultuous times alongside one of my close friends from business school, and knew she'd seen a psychiatrist. I asked her if she recommended him. She did.

The time to act was immediately. And I did. As I've said, indecision is not one of my problems. Ever. My friend gave me the psychiatrist's information and I set up an appointment for the following week.

I told him exactly how things were—that I was spiraling and I couldn't get out of it and that I'd come to understand that I'd been "passing" for years. *Passing* is a term coined by Kenji Yoshino, an expert on diversity and inclusion and unconscious bias who has been on Big Think several times.[1] It means that you are hiding things from others, as opposed to covering, which means people know what's going on but the person downplays the effects.

I'm very good at passing, it turns out. I told the psychiatrist that even in his office I was likely to come off as totally together and reveal very little about myself, but I needed help. I finally did put on my big-girl pants and own my truth. It was time to stop passing.

I asked the psychiatrist if it was time for medication. He, of course, didn't want to rush to conclusions, but for the first time I actually explained precisely how I'd been feeling for months in a nonemotional way. "This is the reality of my every day," I told him. We talked about it for a while, he listened to what I'd been going through, and determined that it would be good for me to get on Wellbutrin.

It takes about ten days to two weeks to take effect, and sometimes the symptoms can become worse before better—you can get more anxious, which can lead to being jittery. For me, that did happen, but not for long. It wasn't as though I was suddenly calm and happy; I just wasn't debilitated. I don't intend to stay on it forever, but I do recognize that if I come off it too speedily, that depression has a way of returning even worse if not treated sufficiently.

So, what does being on the meds mean for me? Am I the picture of calm? No way. But it helped right the ship. I feel as much; I just don't spiral. Would I like to be calmer? Maybe, but that's not me. Some of the discomfort makes me who I am and it gives me an edge. I don't want to be numb, just not in a complete mental spiral unable to see the good. And you know the shame I mentioned earlier about taking action and getting help? The more I leveled with people about what I'd been going through and the fact that I'd gotten help, the better it was. I told friends, family, and even those with whom we were doing business. I can't remember how it came up with one of our clients, but she told me that she'd been going through a rough time and had been really down and had recently gone on meds. I said, "Me, too!" In this business relationship, I was the "vendor," as they say, so it was risky for me. She and I bonded. I've come to realize that showing people who you are and being vulnerable is actually a strength. Allowing people to be compassionate and caring often builds relationships, whether they be business, friendship, or family, and can catalyze closeness.

You don't just get "cured" of anxiety and depression. It's an ongoing thing. Thankfully, I'm self-aware enough to know that I need to work on it constantly. So, I took other measures to help myself. Though completely foreign to me, I started to meditate as part of my effort to realize that while Big Think is important, my mental health and well-being are much more so. I'd be even better if I meditated daily and not in fits and starts, but it is still very helpful when my mind and emotions are getting the best of me. ("Realize, Victoria, it's just a thought. What you are thinking is not really happening. You are okay, right here, right now.")

I reread books on creative visualization—a concept I'd learned about from Shakti Gawain's book *Creative Visualization* before starting Big Think—and began to practice some of the methods. It is true (at least for me) that often, as I think, so shall it be. And, I'm creating the reality around me, at least mentally. Even when I first read the book, it did expand my thinking and get me to loosen up. I think it served as a help when founding Big Think. I utilized the concept of going with the flow as opposed to struggling to make something happen. The river will carry you in the direction, I understood. If you fight against it, you will surely go someplace, but it will be full of struggle and maybe not nearly so good as where you'd have gone if you just relented and let it carry you. I've never thought that means you don't try; it just means that once you are in the river, you need to have at least some faith that it will take you where you need to go. The more you struggle, the more you will suffer, and you'll be less likely to get to a positive destination.

During the course of Big Think, for long periods of time I reembraced the belief that the struggle was important. I needed to struggle, to suffer, in order to actually achieve. And quite honestly, I thought that if people saw me do so, they would have more confidence that I was working hard. Honestly, though, who cares about working hard? I've long said it's the results that matter. But in this instance, with investors and clients, I felt that they expected me to show I was killing myself and sacrificing everything to make Big Think work. This was untrue. And the harder I was working, the more I was clinging to things, the more success, business and personal, was eluding me. There is a Buddhist saying my dad has often shared with me: "Grasp, and it shall surely elude you; open your hands and it may come."

I grasped for much of the time I've run Big Think. It's not joyful. When I've been at my best, I've lived with open hands. Being "in the flow" is just an easier and more pleasant way to be. Example of when I've grasped? Desperately trying to raise money from VCs and individuals over and over.

There was a point in 2013 when things looked really bleak. It felt like we were going out of business. I was desperately trying to figure out any way to get money, and doing so in a very panicked way, which people can see immediately. Chill is the way to be. I hit a wall. I thought, *Okay, then, we're going out of business.* And I had a sense of peace. I literally let go. That same week, I was introduced to a man we'll call Jerry. Jerry is a very successful entrepreneur. After working for tech companies including eBay, he started and sold a company to Alibaba for a whole bunch of money in 2015.

I had literally no expectation of the meeting and just took it out of politeness. Jerry came to our office late one afternoon and we walked down the street for coffee. He had a wonderful, calm energy. He asked me about Big Think and I told him about what we'd built, who was involved, and our struggles. It was as though I were talking to a friend and just being totally straightforward—no attempt to "sell." His questions about the company and about me were exceedingly thoughtful. Then, he asked me what I wanted.

Wait a minute, I thought, *nobody's asked me about me before in the process of starting and running Big Think. This man actually seemed to care about me and my needs. Wow! And he didn't even know me.* We had a very nice time together. He learned about me and Big Think, my family, what I was proud of, what I thought our shortcomings were. I learned about him. After about ninety minutes, we went our separate ways. I left thinking, Well, that was pleasant and he's a good man. I had been "me" the whole time. Not anxious, just real.

The next day, Jerry called and told me he was going to invest $500,000 in Big Think. Whoa. Just when we were desperate for cash and I had not even asked or tried to pitch him. Over the course of the next year Jerry put in an additional $500,000, and a year later got one of his friends to also invest $500,000. He is a man of integrity.

I don't know for sure, but one of the reasons I think he took a chance on Big Think is because he saw my humanity. Yes, he respected what we'd built and the mission, but I feel, most of all, he saw someone honorable and real, trying to make something work. Jerry is on Big Think's board today and is one of my most trusted advisors. I feel if I'd gone into the meeting with him stiff and with a feeling of anxiety and need, the outcome would have been totally different.

TAKING ACTION

Anxiety doesn't just go away, and it's important that I find new ways to combat it and make myself feel better mentally. So, in 2019 I took a drastic step to improve. Picture this: rural Tennessee, May 2019, and the person once dubbed the *Digital Goddess* by David Stern handed in all her devices and attended a weeklong, off-the-grid retreat for self-actualization and learning from others. My friend had told me about Onsite Workshops and how profound it was for him. I was skeptical, but after a tough 2018, that spring felt like a good time to revive. I wanted to examine myself and my relationship with anxiety in a serious way, not just superficially manage it with medication.

This trip was a little out of my comfort zone, to say the least. First we committed to healthy living (as in no alcohol and, for those who use, no drugs) for at least a week before we arrived at Nashville International Airport, where we were picked up in a group bus. It is not a rehab facility; it's a program designed to help you get to your true self and understand the main thing holding you back. Anybody who knows me well knows I am not a "joiner," as my mother would say. I like to be alone, and group activities make me nervous.

When I arrived at the facility, I immediately had my phone and any digital devices taken away from me and was shown to a room I'd be sharing with two other women. I was concerned about how I, someone who cherishes being alone, would fare for six full days and nights with strangers, in an intense daily program of "experiential therapy," which involves group processes including role-playing past and current relation-ships. All meals were eaten together and there was no opting out of anything (of course, I managed to figure out a way to do so—I could only join so much without an escape hatch).

One of the best things I took on board there was the con-cept (and then reality) of examining anxiety. Asking myself the question, *Am I okay right now? Am I in peril in any way?* This was very different than my norm of spiraling into forecasting the doom that was likely to come my way at any point in the future. Bringing my mind back to the here and now was one of the most important lessons of Onsite.

The immersion into experiential therapy started off slowly, to try to ease the tension in the group. We did exercises together to reveal ourselves to the group and help them understand where we came from. To say it was intense is an understate-ment. People discovered things about themselves both by par-ticipating in the exercises and by observing others do them. Imagine spending seven hours a day with nine other people and a therapist in a small room sitting in a circle when the objective is to break down barriers.

I was uncomfortable at first, and my go-to in such situa-tions is humor. That's okay to some degree, but it doesn't truly allow openness. Slowly—I think slower than all the others in the group—I began to feel more at ease. I started to lose the attitude that this was some hokey, self-help, culty thing, and everybody there was crazy (except me).

Later, a woman in my group told me her impressions of me at the start and at the end of the week. She said, "From my perspective when I first met you, you seemed much more quiet and reserved and observed a lot. Maybe it took a minute for you to participate in what was going on. Maybe unsure of it all? But since then, I think you have come out of your shell and have almost sprouted wings like a butterfly. You are not afraid to speak your truth and show the beautiful things you possess inside."

Now, this wasn't my objective, but it sure was nice to hear. My objective was to address my anxiety, and through this experiential therapy, I did. The last exercise involved each of us confronting something that made us anxious, or gave us trauma. There were many unbelievable and upsetting stories to hear, so when I shared my anxiety about running a company and the possibility of letting those who had invested in me and it down, it felt a little, uh, less important. But the group truly listened and gave input and role played, and it was incredibly useful. I did leave with a greater sense of calm. Talking about it all openly with a group I'd come to know well and trust was very meaningful.

The Onsite experience has stuck with me. When I am feeling anxious, I sometimes go back to the notes I took there and some of the information they gave us on difficult relationships, understanding oneself, and codependency, among other things. I had taken real steps to become less anxious, and just by embarking on that journey I made progress. Of course, it's a never-ending battle, but I feel I have more tools to cope now without spiraling.

Did it change me? Yes. I think my family and friends noticed a calmer, gentler Victoria. No fundamental personality transplant, but certainly more centered, and less likely to be always seeing what could go wrong.

The entrepreneurial process is up and down, over and over. In September 2019, the CEO of WeWork was kicked out. Less than a year earlier, the dude was soaring (well, he still is, financially, with an enormous exit package). Things can change on a dime, and if you aren't enjoying the journey, you're missing out. Things *will* change. And being prepared mentally for the ups and downs is something I wish I'd invested in way earlier. If you're looking for a constant high, entrepreneurship ain't your bag. They say it gives you the highest highs and the lowest lows. I can attest to that. And here's the most important thing I've learned: the mental anguish of the struggle doesn't help, and in fact catalyzes more anxiety.

After all is said and done, I've come to enjoy the process—the challenge of living to see another day. I've also come to realize that what drives me, and the people who invested in Big Think, is the mission. We have made people "smarter, faster."

Mental well-being is something many of us need to fight for at least some of the time, but there are times when the need is greater than others. During these periods, it's essential to look inward and examine exactly what needs to change if you are to be successful, both personally and in business. What I now realize is that some of the experiences I've had around this issue have turned out to be blessings. I've addressed long-neglected issues that have complicated my life or made it less enjoyable, like anxiety and trauma. It's been a gift to confront them and get them under control. There are ways to move forward positively. Life, where possible, is to be enjoyed!

REFLECTIONS

◆ Fear not, get help. Mental health is an issue for many; it is not something to be ashamed about.

◆ Enjoy the process. The only thing you have is right now. Enjoy it and don't fear outcomes.

CHAPTER 10

TRYING HARDER TO BE SOFTER

Finding Joy at Work

In September 2019, midway through writing this book, my whole life changed, and so did my mind-set. This was never how I intended to start this chapter or conclude this book, but sometimes life hits you with such brutality that your whole attitude can change overnight.

Earlier in the year, my father had been given the all-clear from Stage 4 cancer and our family breathed a sigh of relief. But on September 5, I received a phone call telling me he was in bad shape, had fast-moving brain cancer, and if I wanted to see him in any kind of lucid state, I needed to board a plane and reach him as soon as possible. My dad has always been the person who encouraged me the most and expected the most from me. As he would describe himself, he's a survivor—a water-from-the-creek, plow-behind-the-horse kind of guy who was brought up in Washington State in the 1930s and '40s in a house without electricity or running water. He did a man's work as a boy. His mother abandoned him when he was two years old, and he ran away to Alaska when he was fourteen to provide for himself and go to school. With all the odds against him, he made a success of himself. And, while he was abused as a boy and had absolutely no idea about love and forming a family, he created an incredibly loving one of his own. I have always looked to him for business and moral direction. And he's been my biggest champion.

Of course, it's never a good time for anybody to die, but this impending loss seemed especially harsh for me. When I talked to my dad on the phone prior to flying out to see him, it sounded like he was falling asleep mid-sentence, but he was making sense. When I arrived, he was in a crowded hospital ward at Toronto General Hospital, designed for urgent care, not long-term stays. I was alarmed. He was sharing a room and a single bathroom with three old, decrepit men, separated only by thin curtains. Dad was being given regular doses of hydro-morph for pain and was pretty much unable to stand. I stayed the whole night with him, sleeping on the floor beside his bed on some hospital blankets. I was deeply concerned that he would fall as he kept trying to get up and move without help. Not a good idea.

I took him to the bathroom several times during the course of the night—not an easy feat with a six-foot-three, 220-pound man (I'm five feet, nine inches, and 125 pounds). It's very upsetting to see your father in that state of abject need, but incredible to see how a human being can adapt to new surroundings and circumstances. I would never have expected my dad to handle a situation like that with the dignity he did. He went from being a fiercely independent, robust man, to being someone who had to be helped to the bathroom, and eventually to have nurses in there with him so that he wouldn't fall off the toilet. The lesson I learned here, and can apply to my own work and life, is that we are resilient and can handle far more than we know. When things are really grim there is a way to work through the pain and struggle with grace and serenity, no matter the circumstance. My dad is a fighter but he moved through this time with a grace that I'd never seen before in him.

I've been going back to see him regularly from New York City as it is very difficult to know how much time he has. We had a conversation in early October 2019 about how he had struggled all his life and been motivated and driven by fear, insecurity, and the need for control. Now, despite being in the most-out-of-control position in his life, he felt calm and happy, and he was not afraid. It was in these truly impossible conditions over the following weeks, coming to terms with my dad's now terminal diagnosis, I made an extremely valuable realization I'll carry with me for the rest of my life: my softness, kindness, and compassion are not what hold me back in life. They're the characteristics that make me stronger. And make us all stronger. Softness in times of duress is strength.

The personal things I've experienced over the last twelve-plus years have softened me as a person and made me a more compassionate CEO. Have I led our company to become a unicorn? Not in the least. Have we created something I and anybody involved with the company value, respect, and even treasure? Youbetya.

Years ago, I would have mostly focused on quantifiable results when measuring the success of Big Think. But there's so much more to measuring value and meaning than numbers, and it's taken a lot of life experience for me to realize that. Now, what I value are the lives we've touched, the wisdom we've shared, the relationships we've formed, the minds we've changed, the careers we've launched or resurrected, the influence we've had in ways we may never know.

Here's the thing—what we learn or experience at work can inform our behavior and attitude far beyond the office. But it's the day to day, and the ups and downs of our personal life, too, and how we respond to them, reflect on them and grow from them, that inform and shape who we are. Some of the personal things I've gone through over the past twelve years have certainly helped me be a better, softer leader. What's the fun in being harsh? I've been that way in the past and not only does it fail to serve the people who are working with me most effectively, it also doesn't serve me. I've come to see that acting tough is actually a form of weakness, and I don't get the best out of myself or my people. There are times when you must let work go and focus on truly more important things. Like those you love.

So, maybe you've got me a little bit by now. I'm only beginning to know myself, and I hope I continue to evolve. I'm a work in progress. Work is a work in progress, no matter where we are. I now recognize my emotions—I can be scared, I can be vulnerable—but what's most essential is that I'm always me. The things that have helped me grow to be softer have actually made me more powerful. I've also discovered that some of the things that I thought made me a "strong" leader were actually making me weaker and less effective.

The average person spends ninety thousand hours at work over the course of a lifetime—that's approximately one-third of the precious time you have on this Earth. And many people work much, much more—as I've done over the last twelve years. Will that time be rich, meaningful, filled with human connection and creative satisfaction? Or will it be routine, dull and impersonal? Work is too central to our lives for it to lack the things that make life worth living.

The idea that we should separate "work lives" from "personal lives" makes no sense to me. And, yet I've done it. Repeatedly over the years. By and large, it's not served me well. Business *is* personal, and we should bring our true self to wherever we are. You don't stop being who you are or what your values are just because the situation changes. And that's something I've taken on board. I'm not two different people depending on the situation—I am the same person, with the same values, no matter where I am. Having the courage to be my authentic self wherever I am is not only good, it makes life more fulfilling for me and for those around me.

I'm intimately involved in the lives of the people who work with me—how could I not be? I'm also intimately involved with the lives of people I don't work with. I'm becoming better at being my authentic self with everyone. It's fundamental to my best life. At least for me, being one person in the boardroom and another (you think you know the next line, but it isn't "in the bedroom") in any other room, just doesn't ring true or make me feel good about who I am. I must be me, anywhere I am. Over the last twelve years of being an entrepreneur and CEO, I've gotten closer to that. Am I fully there? No way. And who knows where I'll be next week, much less the next decade. But being who I am, no matter where I am is, for me, what it's all about. It's taken work and personal growth, development and involved investment in my own training. And, being open to change.

Business literature gives lip service to the importance of "soft skills," but the very term seems to undermine their importance. Love, compassion, care, listening, communicating—these aren't secondary skills. They're of primary importance. Candor and humanity are what I try to bring to all of my business relationships. And that wasn't always the way—hopefully we grow as we experience things. Over the past twelve years I've grown softer in my personal life as well as through many of the experiences I have had at Big Think and many things I've gone through while running it. Yes, my business matters so much to me, and the joy and meaning I've found there is irreplaceable.

But at the onset, and for at least several years into running Big Think, I thought my personal self and my work-self had to be different, that being a leader, especially as a woman, meant showing no emotion, and that being outwardly strong was paramount.

Essentially, I believed that not letting those I work with have a true sense of who I am as a person was the way to be, that letting people in, to know me, was a mistake. I've discovered this to be absolutely not the case. People want to help and be around those who reveal who they are and are transparent about the ups and downs of their lives. Of course, at work, it has to be within the bounds of professionalism, but being professional doesn't mean not being open or clear about your struggles, pain, and failures.

Initially, I only showed my "strong" self, and didn't talk about what was going on in my life personally and certainly didn't discuss the challenges I was facing or my concerns. I've grown so much and have come to see that sharing the very hard times I've experienced with those I work with has helped them understand me and my motivations better, and in so doing, made them want to do better alongside me. And, it's made me kinder and gentler both professionally and in my personal life too. I sacrificed so much of myself to my business, unnecessarily, and let important things slide, as I truly thought personal and business were to be compartmentalized. Not at all.

The journey of building and growing Big Think has been a harder professional road than many others I could have chosen, and the journey of my growth as a human alongside it has been difficult too. But I wouldn't take any of it back. Those struggles, and finally being open about them, have helped me change from having a hard shell to being a compassionate leader. At least most of the time, I hope. It's certainly hard to measure. But those I've worked with over the years have commented that they have seen me grow profoundly in my compassion and ability to lead with softness instead of an iron fist. I think all of the challenges I've experienced, professionally as well as personally, have certainly helped.

In the past, I truly had a hard time saying "I love you" to anyone. Including family. After my experiences in the past decade, I now say it with ease. I'm also much better at putting myself in someone else's shoes. Over the course of Big Think's existence, the intense challenges of being almost out of business several times, letting people go, firing, hiring, and so on certainly took their toll mentally and emotionally, and yet I grew. It was painful, yet I did it.

Here's something I realized along the way: If I am bound to something and scared of failure, it creates a brittleness that will actually attract what I really don't want. It's like my dad used to tell me, if you focus on what you don't want to happen, that's what's going to happen. If I am open, vulnerable, and, yes, soft, it's more likely that I will succeed and those around me will, too, and it will actually be more pleasant for all involved.

Does this mean being a perfect human? Heck, no. I feel with my overriding focus on work, I've let family down over the last twelve years, repeatedly, and I've felt guilty about that. Some of the experiences I've had at Big Think have helped there too. I don't have children, but as many have said to me over the years, which initially I found offensive, I do have a "baby" something I birthed and tended to. And, in so doing, it helped me grow and soften. It's helped me to be clearer, to notice what's actually important in the din of lots of things going on and apply that newfound insight to personal and family relationships as well. No, I haven't been as available as others in my family, as I've also been taking care of my "baby." I may not have created a child—a human child—but I've created *something*. And I hope it has meaning for a lot of people.

VALUES MATTER

Expert insights have also brought about behavioral change for me and running a company like Big Think brings you into close contact with a lot of experts. One of the lessons that affected me considerably was Susan David's interview on values.[1] She said: "*Values* is one of those words we use so often and so loosely that it can lose its meaning. We can start to think of 'values' as something external to ourselves—an organizational marketing mantra or a politically expedient slogan. But knowing and affirming your values is the difference between having a compass to guide you on your path to success and well-being, and being vulnerable to envy, prejudice, and every passing impulse." Bottom line, she says, happiness comes from living your life in accordance with what you value.

This kind of thinking leads me to ask some crucial questions. Have we created something worthwhile at Big Think and would I do it again? The answer is yes. I held true to my values, so despite the company not being a runaway financial success, it has been a public good—and to this day it still is. I've realized that my mission wasn't to get wealthy (although that would it have been nice). I valued helping others and creating something of meaning, and it's been a privilege to do so.

I'm also practicing asking for help. Our board and our investors have been nothing but supportive. Why? I think it comes back to the main point of the book—authenticity. I've been totally open and, in recent years, vulnerable. It's a nicer way to go through life.

FROM FEAR TO FORGIVENESS

Let's go full circle. I began this book telling the story of my arrest, and how I tried desperately to plow through the experience without showing emotion, without anyone knowing how terrified I was. In so doing, I now believe I suffered from post-traumatic stress disorder for more than a decade. I never really got past it until I addressed the situation head-on, having been given an opportunity to be compassionate to the man who had made me feel so afraid.

Compassion may not be received appropriately or well by the person you are dealing with, but it's good for your soul and promotes growth. In 2016, I'd heard that my former employer,

Mr. Snider, had major heart surgery, and I felt an unexpected surge of compassion for the man. I sent him an email after eleven years of absolutely no contact, and he wrote back immediately. In 2017, he faced a different kind of crisis. He was one of the men confronted by the #MeToo movement. He was fired from his job and lost a lot of opportunities. When the press broke the story, I reached out again.

My family and friends thought I was a little nutty, but they have come to understand that I truly don't hold grudges and I believe forgiving people is more beneficial than holding on to anger or, in my case, fear. I would be lying if I didn't say his comeuppance gave me a sense of relief. I finally had some peace that this man could no longer harm me. He'd never abused me in a sexual way, but he had tried to destroy me personally and professionally at a very vulnerable time in my life. "Whatever happens to you, it doesn't take away from the great work you have done. I see that and others see it," I wrote in my email to him. Immediately, he wrote back and asked me for lunch. Silly me, I thought I was going to get an apology.

I arrived at the restaurant—like the good old days, I'd chosen a place I thought nobody would know him—or at least very few. It was a midtown French restaurant in the middle of the week—not exactly a hot spot. Good food but not for the high rollers he was used to hanging around. It was a cold winter's day and I was wearing a black chic coat and my cute little winter tuque, as they say in Canada. I got to the restaurant early, as I always do, and got us a table. About ten minutes later, in walks Snider—all six feet, six inches of him with a long dark coat, and, yes, a large pair of sunglasses on a gloomy, cold day. If he didn't want people to notice him, this wasn't the way. I had to smile to myself.

At first, I was nervous, and seeing him brought back some trauma. I'd seen him a couple times over the years, and it had never been anything but terrifying. This time, I slowly realized as he approached the table, was different. I wasn't scared. I was actually sad for him. A great man, fallen. He came over to me, and, yes, I gave him a hug. I don't think he could believe it. He sat down. I'd ordered a glass of rose and he did the same. This time, he didn't drink mine as well as his. We started to talk a little bit about me, though he never got into anything really personal. He did ask about Big Think. And then he asked—believe it or not—if I knew anyone in my world who could *run his website*. That's right. The man who tried to destroy me and my company was asking me for help. He was also delusional that anybody would want to visit his website, even though he owns all the content from his show.

I was taken aback, but then remembered who I was dealing with. A man completely about himself, all the time. Does this mean he never had moments of kindness? No, he did—and I think it's because I could still see the humanity in him that I was willing and in fact eager to engage, to let the past be in the past and to have closure. But clearly, I overestimated him. Before the lunch, I truly thought he would bring up what had happened years before and apologize, or at least mention it. I knew before the arrest incident that Snider had probably had some fondness, even respect, for me, and it was my hope at this moment that he would recognize that he'd done something to really damage me emotionally and personally. But no. Once the pleasantries were over, he got to the heart of why he actually wanted to meet me. He wanted to know if I knew anybody from my time at his show who had talked to the press. He also wanted to tell me that he had done nothing wrong. If anything, he said, it was a misunderstanding on the part of those who had reported him, and he had only ever been kind to his people.

I sat there and listened. I looked at him and I felt pity. It was almost laughable. He also wanted to let me know that he was coming back, better than ever. And he meant it. I said something like, "I bet." Delusion is a sad thing.

I'd gone to the lunch hoping for some sort of resolution—a clearing of my agony and fear. For more than ten years, I'd lived in anxiety of what this man had tried to do to me, with the help of other powerful men. I thought that it might be an intense conversation, but I was determined to have closure. Guess what? I did. In a totally different way than I'd expected. I forgave this man without him even addressing what he'd done to me. I sat across from him with empathy and sadness for what a lost person he was. There was nothing he could do to me. I was free and I did and do truly wish him well.

We ended the lunch with a hug and him asking me to stay in touch. That was February 2018, and we haven't been in touch since. At that lunch a weight was lifted and through empathy,

I regained my power, my sense of self—one that I should never have lost. After all, I am a Digital Goddess, and nobody can take that from me. It's something I earned in good times and bad times. I approached him at this lunch with softness, and that led to my healing. Being harsh would not have enabled me to let go.

For me, when I am rigid I'm likely to break. And perhaps the same may be true for you. When I'm soft, like a tree that is able to move with the wind rather than snap, it empowers me. To others, the blunt, unmoving approach may seem stronger, but it's the people with the facility to bend and respond flexibly, with softness, who are the ones who actually achieve the most personally and professionally. Giving in also feels really good. You know the feeling when you're in the midst of a difficult work situation or personal issue and you're wound so tight you can barely move? When you just breathe, accept how things are, and don't rail against them and stiffen, new possibilities arise. New ways of thinking about the issue or situation present themselves. Approaching it with ease rather than fear and rigidity allows possibility. It may not work out, but the way of dealing with it is a hell of a lot more enjoyable. Enjoy the process. That's all we have.

I truly don't know what the future holds. The only thing I can control is the way I behave. I don't know what is next for me, but I do know that whatever it is, I will approach the next chapter with vulnerability and softness. And, I go back to the Buddhist adage that my dad loves so much: *grasp and it will surely elude you; open your hands and it just may come.*

REFLECTIONS

- Situations can suddenly change. You can find joy even in the depths of deep uncertainty and when facing what looks like possible demise.

- Bend don't break. Being soft is powerful. You don't need to be "tough" to be an effective leader.

- Bring your real self to work. Being vulnerable can lead to more trusting and empathetic relationships professionally.

- Know your values. Being true to yourself is a critical part of being a leader.

ACKNOWLEDGMENTS

Without Peter Hopkins, this book would not have been written. Peter encouraged me repeatedly over the years to write, and it's thanks to our fifteen-year partnership that I have so many stories and lessons to share. Big Think was Peter's brainchild; without him, there would be no Big Think. Peter has been a friend and partner, a shoulder to cry on in the hard times, and a champion and celebrant in the good. He is without doubt the most important relationship in my professional life. Thank you, Peter, for everything.

What's made Big Think are the thousands of incredible experts—we say thinkers and doers—who contribute their wisdom and make people smarter, faster. I am grateful for all their generous contributions. Thirteen years of working with the extraordinary array of talented people that makes up the Big Think team has helped me grow professionally and personally, and helped Big Think become what it is today.

Putting together and selling a book requires expertise, determination, and chutzpah. I was lucky to be surrounded by a truly excellent team. I thank my agent, Jim Levine, who took on a first-time author and encouraged me to be as truly *me* as I could be. I am grateful to Sara Kendrick, my editor at HarperCollins Leadership, who believed in my story and helped me reach the finish line; and to Ellen Daly, who worked with me and coached me throughout to create cohesion and flow in the stories and lessons.

I am grateful to Big Think's investors and board, especially David Frankel, who led our first round of fundraising to make Big Think possible. He invested in first-time entrepreneurs who had little more than an idea and believed we would make it happen. I thank Larry Summers, whose name and reputation brought immediate viability to our project. Throughout our entire existence, Larry has supported and pushed us to be ever better and has been an essential friend and mentor to me. I thank Alan Yan and Carla Newman, who helped Big Think through challenging times and were always available with their time and expertise.

I thank all those people who encouraged me in my professional journey, especially Bob Ackerman and Mark Nesbit, without whom I would not be where I am today.

I thank my family, who put up with me and believe in me far more than I do myself.

Most of all, I thank my father, Covell Dorn Brown, the entrepreneur after whom I modeled myself. Open your hands, and it surely may come, he taught me.

May his memory be a blessing.

ENDNOTES

CHAPTER 1: NEVER LIE TO YOUR INVESTORS

1. Jesse Itzler, *Living with a SEAL: 31 Days Training with the Toughest Man on the Planet* (New York: Center Street, 2015).
2. "Behind the Numbers: The State of Women-Owned Businesses," WBENC, accessed January 22, 2020, https://www.wbenc.org/blog -posts/2018/10/10/behind-the-numbers-the-state-of-women -owned-businesses-in-2018.

CHAPTER 2: WHO GOES FIRST?

1. Valentina Zarya, "Female Founders Got 2% of Venture Capital Dollars in 2017," *Fortune*, January 31, 2018, https://fortune.com /2018/01/31/female-founders-venture-capital-2017/.
2. Kristin Lenz and Maria Aspan, "Exclusive Report: Hundreds of Female Founders Speak Out on Ambition, Politics, and #MeToo," *Inc.*, September 18, 2018, https://www.inc.com/women-entrepreneurship -report/index.html.
3. Dana Kanze, Laura Huang, Mark A. Conley, and E. Tory Higgins. "We Ask Men to Win and Women Not to Lose: Closing the Gender Gap in Startup Funding," *Academy of Management Journal* 61, no. 2 (2018): 586–614. https://doi.org/10.5465/amj.2016.1215.
4. Brené Brown, "Brené Brown On Shame: The Most Powerful Master Emotion," The Coaching Room, January 9, 2017, https://www .thecoachingroom.com.au/blog/brené-brown-on-shame-the -most-powerful-master-emotion.

5. Katie Abouzahr, Frances Brooks Taplett, Matt Krentz, and John Harthorne, "Why Women-Owned Startups Are a Better Bet," BCG, June 6, 2018, https://www.bcg.com/en-us/publications/2018/why -women-owned-startups-are-better-bet.aspx.

6. Emma Seppälä, "Harness the Power of Calm," interview, Big Think, July 18, 2018, https://bigthink.com/big-think-edge/stay -calm-under-pressure.

7. Emma Seppälä, "Stressed? Use This Breathing Technique to Improve Your Attention and Memory, with Emma Seppälä," interview, Big Think, May 19, 2016, https://www.youtube.com /watch?v=NrJZu6bGyHg.

CHAPTER 3: GROW A PAIR

1. Amy Cuddy, "Amy Cuddy on Authentic Learning and Why You Can't Choreograph Success," interview, Big Think, August 10, 2016, https://bigthink.com/videos/amy-cuddy-on-success -through-incremental-challenges.

2. Amy Cuddy, ibid.

3. Tim Ferriss, "Tim Ferriss: How to break the procrastination spell—for good," interview, Big Think, May 28, 2019, https:// www.bigthinkedge.com/tim-ferriss-how-to-break-the -procrastination-spell-for-good/.

4. Tim Ferriss, from "Tricks for Combatting Procrastination | Tim Ferriss," interview, Big Think, December 6, 2016, https://www .youtube.com/watch?v=4a9GTtTUsIc.

5. Robert Kaplan, from "MASTERCLASS: What Does a Leader Do? With Robert Kaplan," interview, Big Think, November 30, 2014, https://bigthink.com/videos/masterclass-what-does-a-leader-do -with-robert-kaplan.

6. Robert Kaplan, ibid.

CHAPTER 4: GET PERSONAL

1. Amos Tversky and Daniel Kahneman, "Judgment under Uncertainty: Heuristics and Biases," January 1973, https://doi .org/10.21236/ad0767426.

2. Liv Boeree, "4 Professional Poker Lessons to Help You Think Clearly and Live Wisely | Liv Boeree," interview, Big Think, September 11, 2017, https://www.youtube.com/watch?v=FVamrGf8UYA.
3. Liv Boeree, from "Poker rule #1: Your Gut Is Not as Reliable as You Think," interview, Big Think, March 31, 2017, https://bigthink .com/videos/liv-boeree-to-win-at-poker-treat-it-like-a-science.

CHAPTER 5: BOSS NOT B*TCH
1. Robert S. Kaplan, and David P. Norton. "The Office of Strategy Management," *Harvard Business Review*, August 1, 2014, https:// hbr.org/2005/10/the-office-of-strategy-management.
2. Alan Alda, "Alan Alda: Grow Your Empathy Through Better Visual Perception," interview, Big Think, June 8, 2017, https:// www.youtube.com/watch?v=qulq_n5zbTs.

CHAPTER 7: AH, THE ROMANCE
1. Ev Williams. "Formula for Entrepreneurial Success." Medium, October 21, 2014, https://medium.com/@ev/formula-for -entrepreneurial-success-ea0b02c504cd.
2. Pam Belluck, "What Fertility Patients Should Know About Egg Freezing," *The New York Times*, March 13, 2018, https://www.nytimes .com/2018/03/13/health/eggs-freezing-storage-safety.html.

CHAPTER 8: YOUR OTHER MARRIAGE
1. Esther Perel, "Breakfast: Esther Perel on the State of Affairs," interview by Peter Hopkins, Big Think live event, February 22, 2017.
2. Esther Perel, "Is Treating Colleagues Like Friends and Family Possible? Actually, It's Essential," interview, Big Think, March 17, 2017, https://bigthink.com/videos/is-treating-colleagues-like -friends-and-family-possible-actually-its-essential.
3. Lawrence Summers, from "Making Complex Decisions: A Masterclass with Lawrence Summers," interview, Big Think, January 28, 2015, https://bigthink.com/think-tank/larry -summers-making-complex-decisions.

CHAPTER 9: DON'T PANIC!

1. Kenji Yoshino, "Kenji Yoshino on a Pivotal Identity Moment in His Career," interview, Big Think, July 29, 2015, https://bigthink .com/videos/kenji-yoshino-on-accepting-nyus-chief-justice-earl -warren-professorship-of-constitutional-law.

CHAPTER 10: TRYING HARDER TO BE SOFTER

1. Susan David, interview with Big Think, August 11, 2016.

INDEX

dealing with stress, 177–92
 breakdowns, 177–80
 and creating mental stability,
  181–82
 mechanisms for, 184–85
 with therapy and medication,
  182–84
decision making, 110–11, 172
DeLong, Tom, 107–8
denial in codependency, 169–70
Dershowitz, Alan, 58
detaching for inspiration, 112
Digital Goddess, 137
dignity, instilling culture of, 97
discrimination, 118
divorce, 152–53
Dobrovolsky, Kiril, 30–31, 36, 38
Draper, Tim, 26
"dressing to impress," 39–40,
  124–27

E
eBay, 186
Eco Warrior event, 114
Eddy, Bill, 89–90
egg freezing, 155–56
egg retrieval, 151–52, 156
eloping, 147–48
emotions, embracing, 113–15,
  197
empathy, 94, 168, 206–7
employees
 firing, 78, 90–95, 111
 fostering growth of, 112–13
 full-time, 66
 hiring, 78–85
 inspiring, 105
 see also managing people
engagement, 141–46

equity, giving up, 46–47
Errol Morris Interrotron
  method, 67
experiential therapy, 138–89
experts, finding, 34–35

F
failure
 embracing, 64–65
 fearing, 200
 honesty in, 18
 in work vs. relationships, 142
family planning, 150–52, 155–56
Farrow, Mia, 147
Fast Company, 23
fear, 54–57, 75
female bosses, 100
female founders, 23, 123
Fenwick, Lex, 131
Ferriss, Tim, 62–63
"fight or flight," 45
firing employees, 78, 90–95, 111
flexibility, 57–61
forgiveness, 203
Frankel, David, 15–16, 24–25,
  27–28, 146
full-time employees, 66
funding, 39. *see also* raising
  capital

G
Gates, Bill, 112
Gawain Shakti, 185
GE, 48
gender, statistics and perceptions
  based on, 23, 100, 123–24
getting a meeting, 29–30
getting arrested, 1–4, 13–14
Glocer, Tom, 171